LAND YOUR FIRST SOFTWARE JOB FASTER

A Practical Guide for Computer Science Students & Freshers: Resume Tips, Interview Hacks & Proven Job Strategies

*"This book helped **fresh graduates On-Campus** and **Off-Campus get a job** in **no time**."*

RAKESH SINGH

notionpress.com

INDIA · SINGAPORE · MALAYSIA

ISBN 979-8-90510-888-4

Who, What and Why to Read

WHO: Fresh graduates for the **On-Campus and Off-Campus job placements** *in software industries. Best suited for developers and Tester profiles.*

WHAT: Experimented and effective tips and strategies to get you a job in the IT industry. You will learn about mastering resumes, cover letters, getting interview calls, alerts and fear removal, job interview preparations, etc. You will get recruiters insights to help you understand what they are looking for. We'll teach you how to better prepare for job interviews without spending time on the things that don't matter.

WHY: These experimented practical tips & guidance helped fresh graduates on-campus and off-campus get a job in no time.

We tested the tips and strategies from this book on many fresh graduates. All managed to get their first job in less than 4 months, including job preparation. Many tips and strategies are extracted from the mistakes the candidates made during job interviews.

"Being unemployed decreases the chance of getting hired.

Get a job faster!"

Preface

Ready to Learn Experimented Practical Tips and Guidance to Get A Job Fast in The IT Industry?

Here's where you start!

Getting jobs as a fresher or final year student can be frustrating. Trust me, I know. Between hundreds of competitors and rigorous interviews, it seems overwhelmingly impossible. But it's not.

After running my own experiments, I learned three important things.

1. There is no competition. Believe it or not, It's true,
2. anyone can ace the interview,
3. and there are certain tips & strategies that can guarantee success.

I have used these tips to help freshers and final year college students get their dream jobs. **Now I want to do the same for you!**

If you know what recruiters, organizations, and job portals are looking for, scoring your dream job is ten times easier.

In this practical book you will learn:

- 50+ Practical tips to help you get jobs in the IT industry in record time
- Smart strategies to help you prepare for job interviews
- Actionable tactics to get more interview calls
- How to fine-tune Resume and Cover Letters to get noticed
- How to gain the confidence to impress any interviewer

We do not waste time on basic tips like dressing well, arriving on time to an interview, or greeting interviewers. You are smart enough to handle all of that. Rather, we focus on the important and difficult stuff. The real concerns you need help with. The real tips that make a tremendous difference.

Get these experimented practical tips and strategies to quickly secure a promising job in the IT Industry!

Why did I write this book?

For years I have been experimenting to discover how a fresh graduate can get a job in the shortest time possible.

One thing that has always unsettled me is how fresh graduates struggle to get a job. Whenever I saw them striving for a job, standing in longs queues waiting for interviews, asking for referrals, begging for an interview calls, I wondered what I could do to help them get a job quickly. I asked myself why it was so difficult for a fresh graduate to land a job. Was there really an undue competition for entry-level positions in the IT industry?

Indeed, the workforce does not welcome fresh graduates; firms these days seem to care only about the experience and nothing else appears to matter. This breaks my heart as I know that many fresh graduates are talented and just need the right guidance to shine.

I thought I should experiment with my effective ideas, guidelines, and strategies for finding a job in no time. I thus randomly selected a number of fresh graduates on social media who were looking for a job and decided to work with them and see them through until they were gainfully employed. I also made the acquaintance of some final-year students learn about how they could get a job and be well prepared as soon as they got their degree.

Using Skype, I provided them with tips and strategies to land a job, staying in touch with them until they received a job offer. A few months later, they were all gainfully employed in the IT industry, earning a handsome salary, in an admirable position.

From then on, I decided to share my tips and strategies with other fresh graduates who want the same thing — their dream job in their dream firm. This book contains all my strategies to get you employed quickly even as a fresh graduate.

Contents

INTRODUCTION

One thing I have learned is that fresh graduates often find it difficult to prepare for a job interview, especially in the IT industry. They are usually nervous, taking the interview for a challenge or a mountain that they must surmount. This is a normal reaction, as fresh graduates are new to the job market and often naïve. It is a whole other world outside of college, and it is okay to feel lost and confused at first.

From my experience, there seem to be several recurring questions that torment these young people — questions and a lot of "what ifs". What if the industry is already too saturated? What if the competition is too much? What if I don't get the job? What if I don't do well in the interview? What if I mess up in the HR session? How do I get an interview call? What subjects do I have to focus on to pass my interview? So many questions and so much uncertainty.

Understandably, with all these questions and uncertainties, an average candidate can get frustrated and even slip into depression if not properly guided.

If you fall into these categories, or if you relate with some or all of these questions, then it is no coincidence that you are holding this book.

The solutions and answers to your questions are all enclosed in this volume. Here, you will find guidelines and tips, both general and specific, all addressing your problems and questions.

You will learn how to **create an effective resume**, and how to **increase your chances of receiving interview calls**. You will be given significant tips on what you should do **before and after an interview**, how to prepare for the written, technical and HR interviews, and you will also learn how to **overcome the fear of interviews,** which may be holding you back.

One of the greatest challenges of an interview is **how to stand out from the rest** of the candidates. Well, you are in luck here! This book will teach you tips and strategies that will surely make you distinguishable from the crowd, thus landing you an amazing IT job, fast!

By the end of this book, you will have gained significant knowledge, including a better understanding of what it is that companies and firms look for, prior to hiring staff. You will comprehend the **power of the cover letter** in job applications and learn how to draft one to effectively showcase your best qualities.

Think of this as a war — you will be armed with weapons and strategies to defeat the other candidates and win the ultimate prize! You will be well equipped to conduct yourself with the utmost propriety during an interview, meaning you will linger in the minds of the recruiters and get your dream job even faster than you thought possible.

ATTENTION!!!

During the course of this book, you will not find generalist or false overviews on how to land a job as a fresh graduate. **So, there will be no tips like telling you to upskill** with tons of subjects or undertake long-term training in which lots of subjects are taught. None of that stuff.

You may also have heard or read somewhere before that if you want to get a job in the IT industry, you are required to read, master, or adopt certain things. Well, forget it, I will be giving you actual useful tips that work!

You will be given actual practical tips and nuggets that will maximize your chances of getting a job. No generalization here, no erosion of instructions, just simple strategic guidelines that will get you where you should be after college.

This is the ultimate goal: to get you a job in the shortest time possible. If this is what you want, read on, my friend.

CRAFTING WORKING RESUME

Tips you'll learn:

- TIP: Name your resume file properly.
- TIP: Create a good and readable email Id.
- TIP: Build your resume in Word Format, not in PDF.
- TIP: Keep your resume header clear & concise.
- TIP: Write a summary, not an objective with a list of key skills.
- TIP: Include skill-related keywords in the summary and key skills.
- TIP: Present the body content of your resume in the right order.
- TIP: You must describe your role in the college project.
- TIP: Keep your personal details short.
- TIP: Make your resume error-free.

Crafting a compelling and impressive resume is usually the first step toward showcasing your skills to recruiters and getting your desired interview calls while job-hunting.

It's really hard for fresh graduates to create an effective resume that will land them a job quickly.

What most fresh graduates do is copy another person's resume and make small changes to include their own credentials without even thinking about the value of a resume or how it works. Some might even upload it on job portals and expect that this will be enough to make recruiters call them for an interview.

What kind of calls will they get instead?

They will begin to get calls from unrelated sources, offering paid training and internships, and so on. It is very unlikely that a hastily composed resume will ever cause them to receive a call about a job opening at a reliable company. And this may lead to great frustration as time goes by.

But how can a fresh graduate learn how to write an invaluable resume that works well?

Don't worry.

With my tips and guidelines in this resume building section, you will craft the right and working resume for yourself easily and quickly. It will be simpler to create a nice resume if you understand the importance of your resume and how it works.

The primary reason for creating your resume carefully is that you need to showcase the right combination of skills in order to encourage recruiters to interview you.

Below are the main points you should keep in mind to write a perfect resume.

- When recruiters look at your resume, they should be able to spot in a fraction of a second what makes you an exceptional candidate for the job and how you meet **their requirements**. The reason I am saying this is because recruiters will probably have tons of other resumes to read besides yours.

- You need to write your resume in the right way to allow the search engines at job portals (like Naukri and LinkedIn) to find it easily when recruiters search for potential candidates for job openings.

Before moving on to tips on building your resume, I would like to remind you of the reasons why you might get a few or no interview calls. The reasons are:

- Your resume might not look good enough, it may be poorly formatted, causing readability issues.
- Your resume is not being viewed by recruiters.
- The search engines at job portals cannot find your resume.
- Your resume doesn't meet the requirements of the companies. Or your resume does not show your skills and qualities clearly to employers.

Start reading the guidelines and tips to create a perfect resume.

TIP: NAME YOUR RESUME FILE PROPERLY.

It's very important that you give your resume file a readable and proper name, something clear and professional. This will make sure that the recruiters know that the resume is yours.

Personally, I have received hundreds of resumes from the candidates with the file name like 170new.pdf, 1.docx, name-3-resume-mobile.docx, my resume.doc, and so on which is not appreciable.

You must give your resume file a meaningful name and make sure it contains *your complete name with the word resume.*

For example, Rakesh_Singh_Resume.docx.

Right below are some of the "don't" to avoid while naming your resume file:

- Don't use space e.g. Rakesh Singh Resume.docx.
- Don't use version e.g. Rakesh_Singh_resume_1.docx
- Don't append company name to your resume e.g. Rakesh_Singh_Resume_Dell.docx.

Here are some scenarios where the proper naming of the resume file is helpful to the recruiters:

1. With proper naming, the recruiters will know which candidate has which resume. so, tracking it and sharing it with the panel involved in the hiring process would be easier for them.
2. They might be storing the resumes of many people in a folder. So, with proper naming, your resume will be found easily, in the horde of resumes submitted.

- When you send a resume with proper naming technique as an attachment in an email during applying for a job, they can easily find it out of all the resumes submitted.

TIP: CREATE A GOOD AND READABLE EMAIL ID.

This tip explains that you should totally consider creating a good email id that contains your complete name to put on resume header in order to have fluid communication with recruiters.

I have observed that many candidates create email ids that do not match with their names. Sometimes they even create an email id with their nicknames and locations or something different than their name.

Bad email id example:

rockyind9@xyz.com, rakesh.it72@xyz.com, etc.

For now, it is unacceptable for my name Rakesh Singh.

Good email id example:

rakesh.singh55@xyz.com.

Make sure your email id shows your proper name. Suffixing with a number is ok.

With a good email id, it will be easier to tell and confirm your email id to a recruiter over the phone, and they can also find your resume from their stock of resumes easily.

TIP: BUILD YOUR RESUME IN WORD FORMAT, NOT IN PDF.

I have seen many fresh graduates create their resume in PDF format. To tell you the truth, I myself have received many resumes in PDF.

You might be thinking "*what exactly is the problem with the PDF format?*" or "*Why do most recruiters ask for your resume to be sent in Word format?*" Well, below are the main reasons:

Most interviewers will use a laptop to view your resume during the interview. If it's in Word format, they can easily write their comments about you and your interview status on the resume itself and forward it to the next round or level. For this, they need an editable document, rather than a read-only one.

"*The point is that the Word format is easily editable, but PDF is not.*"

Even though some job portals accept PDF, they probably have an option for Word documents as well. I would recommend using the Word format.

Bottom line: *Don't send a resume to recruiters in PDF format* ***unless it is specified.***

TIP: KEEP YOUR RESUME HEADER CLEAR & CONCISE.

Your resume header should mainly contain your name, mobile number, email, and your current address. Below, I have given a bad example of a header and a good one, check it out.

Here Is A Bad Resume Header Example:

This sample is taken from an original resume sent by a candidate.

YOUR NAME

Contact & Address:

Door no: - 1234/45, Mobile: +91**********

Blue Rose Apartment.

Opp municipal school, 123456, Email: r@gamil.com

Mumbai.

Here Is A Good Example:

YOUR NAME	
B-Tech (CSE) 2020	Address: Mumbai
Mobile: +91**********	
Email: r@gmail.com	

You can see the cleanness and readability of the given good example of a resume header. You do not need to write a complete address, just mentioning your city location is perfectly fine, so the recruiters would know your current location. Generally, recruiters prefer candidates from their location to meet them for a face-to- face interview.

TIP: WRITE A SUMMARY, NOT AN OBJECTIVE WITH A LIST OF KEY SKILLS.

You have to capture the recruiter's attention with your resume and tell them why you are the perfect match for their requirement. A summary works better than writing only objectives. Writing merely objective does not help but a descriptive summary does. Some candidates do not even bother to write the technical skills section.

Below is an example of how 90% of fresh graduates write their objective:

> YOUR NAME
>
> B-Tech (CSE) 2020 Address: Mumbai
>
> Mobile: +91**********
>
> Email: r@gmail.com
>
> CAREER OBJECTIVE
>
> To grab an opportunity where I could improve my skills along with the betterment of your esteemed company.

But here is a good example of a summary. This is a summary of a java developer's profile; it was done by a fresh graduate candidate I had guided.

YOUR NAME

B-Tech (CSE) 2020 | Address: Mumbai

Mobile: +91**********

Email: r@gmail.com

SUMMARY

A dynamic fresh graduate filled with the following skills to contribute to a collaborative environment to achieve organizational goals.

- Expertise in Core Java OOPs Concepts.
- Decent knowledge in SQL Database.
- Fluent with Java collection, data structure, and algorithms.
- Passion for learning new technologies and languages.
- Excellent in written and oral communication skills.

TECHNICAL SKILLS

Programming Languages: C, Core Java, SQL, Java Collections, Multithreading, Hibernate, and Spring.

Interest: Data Structure and algorithms.

Database: MY-SQL

It's a no brainer if you compare this nice summary example given and the objective given above it, you can easily decide for yourself which one provides a piece of more comprehensive information about the candidates to the recruiters.

The point I am trying to make is rather than write just a one-line objective, write a brief descriptive summary accordingly with a list of your key skills.

TIP: INCLUDE SKILL-RELATED KEYWORDS IN THE SUMMARY AND KEY SKILLS.

As long as you have crafted a nice resume header, summary, and key skills, make sure you include all the related keywords in these sections for your profile.

Keywords are the words by which a recruiter finds your resume on job portals like Naukri. For example, refer to the summary and skills example given in the previous tip. Java, SQL, Java collection, multithreading, data structure, and algorithms are keywords.

These keywords make it easy for search engines on job portals like Naukri and LinkedIn to find your resume and display it to recruiters when they search for candidate profiles.

For example, if a recruiter puts keywords like "C++" and "algorithms" in the job search engine and you have not mentioned these keywords in your resume, it will be difficult for the engine to locate your resume and place it in front of recruiters.

Below is a snapshot that is taken from my Gmail account. The Naukri job portal writes this on the bottom of the email when a Naukri registered recruiter sends this to you regarding a job opening.

> You are receiving this e-mail because your profile contained one or more of the following words that the recruiter searched on "C#"," C++"," Java"," python", "algorithms"," data structure"

Another scenario you should consider is that an employer has 100 resumes in a repository, and he searches for the keywords and picks the top 10 resumes with the most relevant keywords. If you do not have those keywords, your profile will not pop up for the recruiter. Then you have lost an interview call.

TIP: PRESENT THE BODY CONTENT OF YOUR RESUME IN THE RIGHT ORDER.

This tip explains that the content in your resume should be in the right sequence. so, that the recruiters can easily find related information. The order of a resume body content after header should be arranged from most important to least important content.

Here is a preferable order of the body content of your resume.

1. Summary
2. Technical/key skills
3. Training/Certification
4. Projects
5. Academic qualification
6. Personal Details

NOTE

If you have any work sample online to showcase like online Articles, blogs, projects, and others, you should put them after the key skills. On the work samples, read the Tip "*Showcase your skills and work samples online*" given under the "Stand out from the crowd" section.

Why is the right order of the content important?

Mainly, the recruiters should see the information related to their job requirements first before anything else. Once they find a piece of related information and **halt at your resume**, they will definitely end up reading the other information too.

You realize recruiters see hundreds of resumes on job portals and they receive tons of resumes from the candidates. They have to shortlist a few candidates to take the interviews and because of the volume of their work, they might take only a few seconds to view your resume.

If the important information is not placed first on your resume, the probability of the recruiter skipping your resume is high.

So, you'll miss the interview call, even though you are skilled and deserve the job.

TIP: YOU MUST DESCRIBE YOUR ROLE IN THE COLLEGE PROJECT.

Many candidates write long project descriptions and forget or sometimes outrightly do not bother to write an important point like their role in the project. Recruiters will be more interested in the role you intend to perform in the project. It demonstrates your skills and value to them.

Keep your project description at a length of approximately 3 to 5 lines and focus on writing your role in the project.

Below is an example of a project description taken from a fresh candidate that does not include a role, and the same modified example that includes the role.

Pretend you are a recruiter or in a panel of interviewers. Have a look at these given examples i.e. with and without their role in the projects and think if which tells about the candidates' skills clearly used in the project description.

Example: Project description without Role:

PROJECTS:

Project: Online Travel & Tourism website.

Created a website so that a customer can have to go through the website and choose the desired tour package after registering and payment.

Example: Project description with Role:

PROJECTS:

Project: Online Travel & Tourism website.

Description: Created a website so that a customer can have to go through the website and choose the desired tour package after registering and payment.

Role:

- Responsible for working mainly on the database using SQL Server.
- Coding and Designing webpages using ASP.net, HTML, and CSS.
- Creating a technical document about the project.

By merely looking at the project description and role, a recruiter can easily understand that a candidate is good at a database and have an idea about working on webpages and documentation. ***Doesn't it give a clear picture of the candidate skills gained during the project to the interviewer?***

Bottom line: Add roles to all your projects done.

TIP: KEEP YOUR PERSONAL DETAILS SHORT.

You should keep your personal details limited in your resume. You do not have to make your resume so complex, let it remain clean. During shortlisting of resume, generally, no recruiters are interested in reading your personal details.

The example below is enough.

PERSONAL DETAILS:

Father's Name :

Language Known :

Date of Birth :

Your Name

Do not overload it with too much information such as the mother's name, current address, and permanent address, etc. as an example given below.

PERSONAL DETAILS:	
Name	:
Father's Name	:
Mother's Name	:
Sex	:
Nationality	:
Language Known	:
Present Address	:
Permanent Address	:
Contact No	:
Date of Birth	:
	Your Name

Once you are hired, companies can take all your details.

It should also be noted that a declaration section is not required to be put in your resume. You will probably sign the declaration if you are hired by the way.

For example,

I declare herewith solemnly that all the above information is accurate to the best of my knowledge.

Your Name

TIP: MAKE YOUR RESUME ERROR-FREE.

This cannot even be overemphasized, make sure your resume is error-free. Check for any spelling and grammatical mistakes or wrong words like using 'sale' instead of 'sell' in your resume.

If there is an error in your resume, then the claim that you have good oral and written communication skills has been violated. It also diminishes your first impression, in an interview or during the resume shortlisting process.

The best tool to make your resume error-free, in my suggestion is "*Grammarly MS Office® Plug-in*". The free version of this does most of the work. You can find other tools over the internet if you wish.

Personally, I use Grammarly when I update my resume or write some articles.

Bottom line: Correct all spelling and grammatical mistakes from your resume!

To round up this part, here is a sample of a GOOD RESUME for a FRESH GRADUATE.

YOUR NAME

B-Tech (CSE) 2020 Address: Mumbai

Mobile: +91**********

Email: r@gmail.com

SUMMARY

A dynamic fresh graduate filled with the following skills to contribute to a collaborative environment to achieve organizational goals.

- Expertise in Core Java OOPs Concepts.
- Decent knowledge in SQL Database.
- Fluent with Java collection, data structure, and algorithms.
- Passion for learning new technologies and languages.
- Excellent in written and oral communication skills.

TECHNICAL SKILLS

Programming Languages: C, Core Java, SQL, Java Collections, Multithreading, Hibernate, and Spring.

Interest: Data Structure and algorithms.

Database: MY-SQL

WORK SAMPLES (If any)

TRAINING/CERTIFICATIONS (If any)

PROJECTS:

Project: Online Travel & Tourism website.

Description: Created a website so that a customer can have to go through the website and choose the desired tour package after registering and payment.

Role:

- Responsible for working mainly on the database using SQL Server.
- Coding and Designing webpages using ASP.net, HTML, and CSS.
- Creating a technical document about the project.

ACADEMIC QUALIFICATIONS

PERSONAL DETAILS

Father's Name :

Language Known :

Date of Birth :

Your Name

NOTE:

1. You will read about work samples in the incoming tip "*Show Case Your Skills and Work Samples Online*" under the section "STAND OUT FROM THE CROWD"
2. If you really want to be specific with some profiles such as Testing profiles or others, you can use the same resume format. Especially, you need to focus on composting the SUMMARY and TECHNICAL SKILLS accordingly.

A FINAL NOTE ON CRAFTING YOUR AWESOME RESUME.

So far you crafted a good resume, here are some basic final notes.

1. If you've written an article on any website or have written a press release or have any work sample/real project, and so on that, you have kept on GitHub repository or somewhere, please mention their links after the KEY SKILLS section in your resume.
2. If you really want to write some achievements acquired during college such as an editor, dance award and so on, I recommend writing to them after education qualification. Because recruiters have very little interest in those kinds of achievements.
3. In general, hobbies and declaration are not required. I would advise you not to write them down.

Congratulations!!! You are done with creating your awesome and working resume that adds values to both the recruiters and job portals search engine.

Bonus Tip:

Every time you update your resume, email a copy of your resume to yourself, so you can always have the latest version in your inbox.

I have observed that whenever I asked for an updated resume to candidates, their answer was that "the laptop was broken down or they forgot the folder name. so, they ended up losing their resume, etc."

So, I found that emailing the latest copy of the resume to self was the best option to keep the updated resume safe.

INTERVIEW CALLS BOOSTER

Tips you'll learn:

- TIP: Fill out your profile properly on job portals.
- TIP: Use a concise email cover letter for a job application.
- TIP: Log in to job portals regularly.
- TIP: Consider buying paid services from the job portals to get interview opportunities.
- TIP: Ask your friends/relatives for a referral.
- TIP: Visit company sites and upload your resume to their career section.

Now, most recent graduates believe that having a resume is all it takes to land and secure a good job.

Regardless of whether you have already crafted a resume that works well with recruiters and job portals, this chapter goes in-depth and further explains some strategies to give an extra boost to the visibility of your resume and get you to be invited for interviews faster.

You want your resume to have a wide scope, an extensive reach, and a broad spectrum to resonate with all types of recruiters. If your resume does not achieve a more comprehensive level, it will not perform at its best, resulting in fewer interview calls, which will delay you in getting a job.

In order to give your resume some extra visibility, you need to perform some tasks regularly while searching for a job. Getting those interview calls faster is your ticket to landing a good job, and this chapter reveals the secrets. You should not miss a single opportunity during your job hunt, as it is a crucial time for your career.

NOTE

It should be noted that the tasks mentioned in the tips, despite requiring an ongoing effort, should not take much of your time.

The two tips recorded here — (1) *fill your profile information properly on job portals* and (2) *use a concise cover letter for a job application* — demand a one-shot effort. You can put some time into writing a remarkable cover letter that you can re-use several times by making minor changes to conform to the requirements of each job opening.

TIP: FILL OUT YOUR PROFILE PROPERLY ON JOB PORTALS.

First of all, you should upload your resume as many job portals as you can. Job portals like such as shine.com, monster.com, indeed, Naukri and LinkedIn, etc. and any other available in your country.

According to my observations, in India, the Naukri and LinkedIn have been very effective towards getting interview calls, and, it is very important that you should never forget to upload your resume to these two job portals. Personally, I have been using only the Naukri.com for years and its working nicely for me.

Now, the most important part of actually uploading your profile on these job portals is, filling the information in the profile section on all the job portals properly.

Generally, candidates just upload their resume and do not bother to fill their information properly thinking it's just the resume that matters when actually, the recruiters first see the relevant profiles on the job portals itself. And it is your profile that will compel them into downloading your resume.

If you have a bad profile or a badly filled profile with incorrect information, the recruiters might just bypass your profile altogether. A bad profile makes it very difficult for the recruiters to find information related to their job requirements and shortlist your resume unless they download your resume. So, most likely you are going to miss the interview calls.

Filling proper information's about your profile on the job portals will not only help recruiters but will also help the job portal's search engines to find your profile easily. When a recruiter search for a relevant candidate's profile, the search engine pops out the best profiles first with the help of information provided on the portals.

TIP: USE A CONCISE EMAIL COVER LETTER FOR A JOB APPLICATION.

In this tip, you will learn what a cover letter is and its importance. You will also see a bad and a good sample of a cover letter and guidelines for creating it well. A cover letter is one of the key ingredients to getting interview calls and leaving a good impression on recruiters that will boost your chances of getting hired.

Whenever you are applying for a job or sending an email to a recruiter, it is beneficial to write a concise cover letter and attach your resume.

Here is a brief overview of what a cover letter is.

> A cover letter for a fresh job seeker typically contains your key skills, certifications, and training if any. It mainly shows how you would be helpful to an organization. If you have something online to showcase like blog articles, projects, and published papers, you should provide the links also. (check out the email cover letter sample for a fresh graduate below).

Imagine that you have received an email for a job opportunity from a recruiter, and you need to reply to him with your resume.

How would you apply?

A majority of fresh candidates just reply with the statement, "*Attached to this email is my resume*", as given below. That's it. This is really a bad example of an email cover letter.

Subject: the subject line.

Dear Sir/Madam,

Attached to this email is my resume.

Best Regards,

Name:

"You must write a cover letter when you apply or reply to a job application."

Isn't it better to write a cover letter instead of just writing "*Attached to this email is my resume*"? Don't you think that a recruiter is more likely to open your resume out of 100 other emails if you have written a cover letter?

For a moment, pretend you are a recruiter. Out of 100 emails from different candidates, which one would you be interested in: one with a cover letter, or one without?

It is important to always write a good email cover letter and attach your resume. On some job portals you will also have an option to write a cover letter, so please do not forget to do so.

Bottom line: A cover letter is one of the key ingredients for getting an interview call.

Check out the good email cover letter sample next. You will find two cover letter samples here, one for a developer profile and another for a testing profile.

Cover Letter Sample – Developer profile

Subject: Fresher- Interest in Java Developer Profile

Dear Sir/Madam,

I'm a BE-2020 (CS) fresh graduate highly interested in the job profile in your company.

I have expertise in Java programming language and fluent with basic skills in C, C++, SQL. Love data structure and algorithms. I have implemented my college project using java and SQL successfully being in the role of developer. I love coding, data structure, and algorithms.

I have taken training in (your topics) from (where). (Training/ Certification if any)

It would be a great opportunity for me to prove myself and contribute in a collaborative environment to the growth & success of the reputed organization.

Best Regards,

Name:

Mobile:

Email:

Cover Letter sample – Testing profile

Subject: Fresher- Interest in Testing Profile

Dear Sir/Madam,

I'm a BE-2020 (CS) fresher highly interested in the job profile in your company.

I have excellent knowledge in Java programming language, SDLC, and fluent with basic skills in C, C++, SQL, data structure and algorithms. I have a basic idea of manual and automation testing.

I have implemented my college project using java and SQL successfully being in the role of developer & tester. I love finding faults in software applications.

I have taken training in (your topics) from (where). (Training/ Certification if any)

It would be a great opportunity for me to prove myself and contribute in a collaborative environment to the growth & success of the reputed organization.

Best Regards,

Name:

Mobile:

Email:

IMPORTANT NOTE ABOUT A COVER LETTER AND GUIDELINES

NOTE

- If you have received an email from a recruiter with a subject line. Please don't change. Just hit the reply and write your cover letter.
- You must write the subject line if you are writing a fresh email for a job application to a recruiter.

GUIDELINES FOR WRITING A COVER LETTER

Refer to the above sample and write your cover letter in the following order.

1. Never forget to write the subject line while applying for a job with a cover letter. If you are replying, the subject line must be there and no need to write.
2. Write your degree, year, and interest in the mentioned job profile.
3. Write your technical skills related to your profile, role in project's done, and interests.
4. If you have done any training or certifications, then include them.
5. Write about your achievements and pieces of evidence (e.g. online blog, published paper, any profile related online documents, etc. You can provide the link).
6. Write a finish line something like as shown in the sample – "It would be a great opportunity...)
7. Correct all spelling and grammatical mistakes from your cover letter.

TIP: LOG IN TO JOB PORTALS REGULARLY.

Try to update or login to the job portals e.g. Naukri and LinkedIn at least, every day. You need to be serious and must do this activity to get interview calls.

This is necessary because, due to this activity, the job portals search engines, and the recruiters will get to know that you are still looking for a job. It means your job status will be visible to the recruiters that are if you are still looking for a job.

If you don't follow this activity, the recruiters may either bypass you or not even contact you entirely as they may think that you might have already got a job or is no longer you are looking for one.

Recruiters and the algorithms of job portals both notice candidates who have been active lately. Recruiters are interested in calling those who have visited job portals most recently because they don't want to waste time and money calling people only to check if they're looking for a job. So, obviously, recruiters and the search engines at job portals will prioritize you if you view and update your profile regularly, as this indicates that you are still looking for a job.

Also, the job portals search engines tend to make your resume gradually drop from the top, and at some point, **it will disappear** if you do not visit and update the job portals regularly.

It should be noted that a candidate who has updated his resume recently will stay at the top and will easily be accessible to the recruiters.

Login/update your profiles on whichever Job Portals you use every day before 9 AM because, recruiters usually start looking for profiles when they start their job at the office and by doing this, they may find your resume on top.

TIP: CONSIDER BUYING PAID SERVICES FROM THE JOB PORTALS TO GET INTERVIEW OPPORTUNITIES.

Most people do not do this, but you should consider buying a paid service from the job portals that give you interview calls. Check out if this kind of service is available on the job portals. It gives an advantage over others.

For example, the Naukri.com provides the paid services such as display resume & recruiter connections to get interview calls. You can find similar services available in your country on job portals.

Warning:

Now, referring back to the tips I gave on including keywords to your resume, It should be noted that, if your resume does not contain related keywords for the kind of job you are looking for, it will be a waste of money to buy services as their search engines will not be able to display your resume to the recruiters when they search job seekers profiles using keywords. So, the display resume kind of service will not be so effective. These services are an extra opportunity to get interview calls, but before buying one, make sure you have done all the right things first.

TIP: ASK YOUR FRIENDS/RELATIVES FOR A REFERRAL.

This next tip under how to increase job interview calls, basically suggests that you ask your relatives and friends working in an IT Company to refer or recommend your resume to their company in case of any vacancies.

In the inside referral, there is a maximum chance for an interview invitation and getting hired. Because, first of all, you get a genuine interview and the company trust you because of their employee. If you do not have any friends or relatives working in an IT company, it is not exactly something to worry about as this was just another way to take your resume to the companies.

A side note: In case you are wondering if asking referrals on social media like Facebook, is a good idea, it's not. It is better to avoid that because you could end up falling for a scam. It's better not to waste your time on something like this. But if you do have friends that are genuine on social media then it could be okay.

Bonus Tip:

Connecting with other candidates during walk-in or an interview you go for is a good idea. Other candidates might be part of some job groups or they might know of some other interviews. So, try to stay in touch with them regularly.

TIP: VISIT COMPANY SITES AND UPLOAD YOUR RESUME TO THEIR CAREER SECTION.

Find the list of companies and visit their websites (search company list on google). On their website, you should find the career section. Check if there is any specific requirement for application or just simply try to upload your resume.

Many companies also have their own job search facility on their website. You can find the current opening matching to your skillset and apply it.

For your information, this tip may not be very effective as many companies hire consultants to recruit candidates. But there is still a chance to look at your resume and give you a call. So, take the opportunity.

Bonus tips:

Find start-up companies in your location and visit their website. apply in their career section. Since they are a start-up, they may not want to invest money on a consultant for the hiring process, and chances of interview calls are high.

FOCUS WORDS

1. Having a clear and concise summary of your profile is essential; using keywords and having a well-presented cover letter are the most important ingredients for obtaining interview calls.
2. Ensure your expertise topics are at the top of your resume summary and list down all of your skills under 'key skills,' this will get the recruiters' attention immediately.
3. The keywords i.e. your skillset, are the most important components to focus on regarding job portals. By focussing on this area, job portals will quickly locate your resume, and refer it to the recruiters when they search for potential candidates who meet their job requirements.

DURING A TECHNICAL INTERVIEW

Tips you'll learn:

- TIP: Prepare for the question "tell me about yourself".
- TIP: Make eye contact and treat the interviewer as your friend.
- TIP: Bring two copies of your resume to every interview.
- TIP: Don't let your phone interrupt the interview.
- TIP: Listen carefully to the interviewer's questions.
- TIP: Include examples in all your answers.
- TIP: Answer a question completely.
- TIP: You must try the coding problems given in the technical interview.
- TIP: Don't argue with the interviewer, and learn to say, "I don't know".
- TIP: Be careful when answering "Do you have any questions for me?".
- TIP: Don't ask for the result after the interview is done.

Now, after crafting a killer resume and boosting your interview invitations, it is extremely important to learn and understand the important aspects, technicalities, strategies, and precautions to keep in mind in order to wow your interviewers.

From my experience, I have realized that fresh graduates struggle with interviews, not knowing how to act, what to say, and how to respond to some strategic questions with equally strategic answers.

It is essential that a fresh graduate learns this. I have served on technical interview panels at top-notch organizations and I often noticed the little things that fresh graduates did wrong at interviews. In this chapter, these things will be corrected, and you will be on your way to a successful interview.

Extra focus:

Although all the guidelines and tips explained in this section are extremely helpful and equally important for you to succeed in an interview, I suggest that you give special attention to the following tips:

Include examples in all your answers, *Prepare for the question "tell me about yourself"*, and *Be careful when answering "Do you have any questions for me?"*

You should get ready for the questions "*Tell me about yourself" and "Do you have any questions for me?"* **in advance** because these are common questions in interviews. I am going to reveal a strategic way to approach these questions and wow the panel. Accordingly, you should write down your answer and put it to good practice by talking to yourself.

TIP: PREPARE FOR THE QUESTION "TELL ME ABOUT YOURSELF".

This is a common start-up question at interviews. You can be sure that it will almost always be asked. In your answer, you **should not** include your educational qualifications or grades, **but** the skills you have acquired that add value to companies. You should also talk about projects you have worked on and what your role was. Go on to describe your area of interest and so forth. Also, if you have any work samples online, such as articles, project pages, etc. (details *in tip: "Showcase your skills and work samples online"*), don't forget to tell them about it.

Make a special note: Please don't include family background information when you are introducing yourself: for example, things like "*I have two brothers and one sister,*" "*We live in XYZ city,*" or "*My father works in XYZ company*". One exception to this rule would be if such information is specified, then you should describe it.

Here are samples of a bad and good answer to the question "tell me about yourself". I would recommend you prepare your introduction, accordingly, write it on paper and practice speaking it.

Interviewer: Tell me about yourself.

Bad answer example:

> Sir, my name is X. I have completed BTech from Y college. I am from Mumbai. I have two brothers and a sister, and my father is a government employee, and mother is a housewife. I know C and C++ and my hobby is to play cricket.

Do you think there is anything in the above introduction to lure the interviewer? Let me show you a good example.

Good answer example:

> Well, I graduated with a degree in Computer Science. I chose that field of study because I have always been interested in the programming & technology world. I have expertise in java programming language and have basic skills in C, C++, SQL. Also, I successfully implemented my college project using Java and SQL. I love coding and algorithms. I also love following technical websites and books, and I have a learning attitude. I write about multiple technologies on the website xyz.com.

TIP: MAKE EYE CONTACT AND TREAT THE INTERVIEWER AS YOUR FRIEND.

Of course, it's understandable that you feel nervous in interviews, but whatever you do, do not let it show. There is nothing more awful than a candidate who doesn't seem confident. Interviewers generally do not consider people like this, so it's important that you avoid it. Besides, letting your nervousness through will negatively affect your performance.

Eliminating nervousness even boils down to intricate details about how you portray yourself, your appearance, and how you speak.

So, what must you do to get rid of nervousness?

Here's a secret strategy that you can use when being asked questions. Rather than just answering them, learn to 'discuss' them instead keeping smile on your face. Imagine the interviewer as your friend, who wants a piece of your knowledge. You wouldn't go straight to the answer if you were talking with your friend, would you? This is exactly why this is a proven strategy. It'll drastically improve your confidence and you'll come off as someone who's focused and knows what they are doing.

Let's do a small exercise, shall we?

Just close your eyes and imagine a close friend of yours is sitting across from you. This friend asks you a question. Now with your eyes still closed, consider how you would respond to the question.

Try it NOW and see.

Welcome back! That wasn't so hard, was it? You see that you weren't nervous or fidgety. You answered with confidence and discussed the answer. Use this method to imagine an interviewer asking the same question. Now answer exactly as you would if he were a friend. It's as simple as that, no rocket science involved.

However, it is important to note that treating the interviewer as a friend doesn't mean you should be too casual. It doesn't mean that you should use informal language like ''bro'' ''hey'' or ''what's up''.

That's not advisable. You can be friendly and yet still sound formal, you can be at ease and address them as Sir or Ma'am. You can even address them by their names if they don't mind, but Sir or Madam is more advisable.

Also, do not confuse confidence for pride and arrogance. There is a fine line between them. Do not cross it.

TIP: BRING TWO COPIES OF YOUR RESUME TO EVERY INTERVIEW.

Take two copies of your resume when you are heading for an interview: one copy for HR and another for yourself.

Having a copy to yourself is not only beneficial and acceptable but having it in front of you for your reference as you discuss your skills makes you look prepared and professional.

What are the reasons to bring another copy, you might ask? Below are several:

During the interview, you might need to explain some answers with examples or diagrams. Generally, there is a stock of paper available on the interview table for you to write answers, but what if there is none? Are you going to say, "*Sir, I want my resume back so I can explain my answer with an example or with a diagram*"? Possible, but it sounds awkward. However, if you have a personal copy of your resume with you, you can start using it.

Also, the interviewer may not allow writing on his copy of the resume, as that may be where he would write his own notes concerning your interview.

Without a paper to write on, you might not be able to give your best answers, and the interviewer might just want to move on to the next question after listening to the concept without any example, details, or visual representation of your answer. (*There will be more tips in later parts that will show you why you should provide examples/ diagrams to answer questions in the interview.*)

Another reason why you should have a copy of your resume is that, if someone referred you to the company for an interview, you can write down the reference details (i.e. name, contact information, etc.) on your copy beforehand. This is helpful because the interviewer or HR may ask you. If you have written these down, you can quickly give them. It doesn't make a good impression to say that you will provide the information later or start searching for a contact on your phone.

However, the first reason mentioned above is the main one for having a second copy of your resume.

TIP: DON'T LET YOUR PHONE INTERRUPT THE INTERVIEW.

It speaks negatively of you if your phone rings during an interview. It is always better to keep your phone in silent mode when you are attending one, as the ringing will distract and disturb both you and the interviewer. You may be busy writing things like logic and algorithms, or maybe delivering or discussing an answer, and your phone rings. This can be very distracting.

In situations where you forgot to put your phone in silent mode, in case it rings, it is polite to make an excuse and switch your phone off or put it on silent mode.

Note that, in general, interviewers are quite flexible. They would not mind your phone ringing once and would rarely take it as a reason for rejection.

Regardless, it is better to just put your phone on silent mode before the start of an interview. It's what I do personally.

TIP: LISTEN CAREFULLY TO THE INTERVIEWER'S QUESTIONS.

Listen properly and understand well before you answer any question an interviewer is going to throw at you. Never interrupt until he is done with the question.

For example, a candidate of mine made this mistake. When the interviewer was writing a coding problem on paper, he poked his nose in and said, "Sir, I already know this problem and the solution". This behavior shows that the candidate does not have good listening skills and in industry, this is considered very bad practice. You might be familiar with a similar problem or the same one, but can you really know what the question will be before it's finished?

However, it is not wrong to ask that the question be repeated if you do not understand it the first time. It is only proper to ask again rather than answer something you have misunderstood. Many fresh candidates think that asking for a repetition of the question will affect the interview, but that is not true.

In reality, it demonstrates that you have a habit of making sure you understand requirements before proceeding. You already know that if you are clear on the requirements, you will do it fast and accurately.

TIP: INCLUDE EXAMPLES IN ALL YOUR ANSWERS.

When an interviewer asks you a question, don't respond with just a plain definition or a single sentence. You should always use an example to illustrate your answer. You already know that examples help people understand a concept better, but this is a gentle reminder. I have observed that most fresh graduates did not give conceptual examples during the technical interviews I attended.

For example, if the interviewer asks, "What are a class and an object?", then answer with the definition, describe, and demonstrate code examples. Get a paper and pen and show the interviewer how a class is written, how an object is created, and any more points you remember.

It is good to pretend that the interviewer does not know anything about it like you are speaking to a layman. You should answer every question with examples, code, or by using diagrams if possible.

It should be noted that **the interviewer may not ask you** for an example and just ask for the concept. Still, make sure you are giving a nice example besides the concept.

Bonus tip:

It is very difficult to recollect or compose examples for the conceptual questions on the fly, especially when you are in front of an interviewer, so please prepare examples for every concept related to the topics beforehand. Better still, have a record of these examples in the form of a note. This will help you in every interview and also as a quick revision.

For instance, you can write a good interface example with code, abstract class, method overloading, and so on.

TIP: ANSWER A QUESTION COMPLETELY.

If an interviewer asks a question like, "*what is polymorphism?*", a fresh graduate's answer is usually "*one entity with many forms is known as polymorphism*". And that's it.

However, imagine that you don't know the concept of polymorphism. *If I simply answer that it is an entity with many forms, would you completely understand what polymorphism is?* Certainly not. So, if you cannot understand the statement, then how can an interviewer understand? He will immediately think that you don't know the concept.

The golden rule is, *if an interviewer asks about concepts from any topic, you should answer with everything you know until he stops you and says it's ok before moving to another question.*

This is an example:

Interviewer: What is polymorphism?

As an acceptable answer:

You should give the definition of polymorphism, then tell him what the techniques are to achieve it, such as constructor and method overloading, method overriding, etc., all with pseudo-code examples. Tell him about compile time and run time polymorphism and anything else you know. ***The point is to answer as much as you can.***

TIP: YOU MUST TRY THE CODING PROBLEMS GIVEN IN THE TECHNICAL INTERVIEW.

Sometimes it happens that as soon as the interviewer asks for a coding problem, the candidate immediately says, "*Sorry, I can't solve it.*"

I would recommend that you at least give it a try, think it over. You may actually be able to crack it. **If you require more clarification about the problem or a hint, ask the interviewer.** For example, if he asks you to *check if a string is a palindrome* and you do not understand what that means, you can ask the interviewer "*What is a palindrome?*" There is nothing wrong with that, and it cannot be a reason for rejection. He ultimately needs a solution from you, after all.

Try to place your logic first rather than jumping straight to the code. **If you can crack the logic, there is a chance that you can write the code as well.** If you are not able to write good code but can find the logic, or if you write code with errors, that's fine. It's still a plus point in the interview and it is better than an outright **NO.**

NOTE: It should be noted that **asking questions to the interviewer for clarification if needed to solve a problem is always a plus point.** It shows that you do not jump into a problem without understanding it, but instead, you think about its logic before coming up with the best solutions.

The reason why interviewers appreciate it when you ask them for clarification is that understanding and consolidating the requirements is one of the most difficult parts of a project.

If you have this habit, it will help a company develop cost-effective projects at a faster rate. In simple words, if you have a clear understanding of a problem, you can solve it more efficiently and quicker.

Bonus Tip:

Keep your voice ON while writing the logic and solving the problems, so that the interviewer can clearly understand what you are thinking of with your approach. If the interviewer feels something is wrong or sees that you are facing difficulties, he can provide you a hint to solve the problem.

TIP: DON'T ARGUE WITH THE INTERVIEWER, AND LEARN TO SAY, "I DON'T KNOW".

Sometimes, interviewers may disagree with something you said or an answer you gave. Under no circumstance should you argue with them or try to prove you are right.

If they disagree with an answer you gave, just let them know that the answer is accurate to the best of your knowledge, but you stand corrected and will research to be certain.

Interviewers are always impressed by this; it means you are teachable and can be corrected. It means that you are a team player that understands other people's opinions and viewpoints and will do all it takes to complete an assigned project or task.

Also, and this is very important, do not be afraid to admit you do not know the answer to a question. Admitting your ignorance is totally fine. No man is an island of expertise and admitting your lapses in knowledge may impress an interviewer. Besides, admitting it is better than acting like you know when you do not. Acknowledging that you do not know the answer to a question does not necessarily mean you will be rejected. Remember that.

TIP: BE CAREFUL WHEN ANSWERING "DO YOU HAVE ANY QUESTIONS FOR ME?".

Usually, if an interviewer asks, "*Do you have any questions for me?*" at the end of the interview, most candidates just reply with a straight NO.

Please do not say NO.

This is a really bad practice, you should never just up and say "NO".

You should always ask questions, very good ones. This is an extra opportunity to impress the interviewer.

Here are some impressive examples of questions you can ask the interviewer.

- What are your expectations from me if I am selected?
- What kind of projects or products does this company provide?
- What platforms does the company use for projects/ products?

This type of question shows that you are not only interested in the company and what it does, but you are also anticipating working with them. This reveals your good mindset to the interviewer, which is in itself an added value to the interview.

You should make note of the below warning:

Never ask questions about holidays and how long the leaves are in the organization. Regarding your salary, you can discuss this with HR and not with the interview panel, unless the panel brings up the salary themselves.

TIP: DON'T ASK FOR THE RESULT AFTER THE INTERVIEW IS DONE.

One of the mistakes that candidates make is asking the technical panel or interviewer the following questions immediately after the interview:

- Sir, am I selected for the next round?
- Ma'am, how was my interview?

Asking these types of questions is not just wrong but immature. It may also give the interviewer the feeling that you are desperate.

Generally, there is no need to ask these kinds of questions as it will not change the outcome. If the interviewer finds your interview good, you will surely get a positive result.

In some interviews, you will get an immediate answer. The interviewer may ask you to sit outside and HR will let you know the status of the interview if you are selected for the next round.

This is also true if the interviewer is impressed with your skillset. Sometimes he may indicate or tell you clearly that you have made it into the next round of interviews, but not necessarily.

Rather than ask these questions, I would recommend that you just say "thank you sir/madam" after the interview.

AFTER A TECHNICAL INTERVIEW

Tips you'll learn:

- TIP: Recollect and write down key points and questions from the interview.
- TIP: Don't wait for your interview results.
- TIP: Do not decide for yourself the reason for your rejection if you are not accepted.

The inner battle fresh graduates go through after an interview is another struggle in itself.

After many rounds of interviews, fresh candidates either get a job offer or become clearly aware that they are being rejected.

When the HR personnel says, "We will get back to you," this statement could have different meanings. It could mean you may be rejected and may never be called back, or it could mean they will get back to you very soon.

None of these meanings ensure rejection or selection though. You may be offered a job later, but not necessarily.

Candidates who do not receive a call are very likely to become sad and fall into depression. They may feel that they did not do well in the interview and jump to the conclusion that they have been rejected. This can also lead them to think that their marks are low, or they have poor communication skills, or an education gap, etc. A lot of misleading thoughts may take over their minds, in fact. It has been observed that many fresh graduates, left to their own devices, will decide upon a reason to explain their rejection in an interview, such as poor communication or low grades.

Those who do not receive a call soon after an interview and think his interview was good may also begin to indulge in unproductive activities while they spend days, weeks, or even a month waiting to be contacted. They may put aside any further preparation for job interviews, and decide to relax, watching films, chatting, using social media, etc.

This topic is going to present some practical tips on **how to handle yourself after an interview**, and how to be super productive in order to attain your first dream job faster.

TIP: RECOLLECT AND WRITE DOWN KEY POINTS AND QUESTIONS FROM THE INTERVIEW.

After your interview, it doesn't matter whether you feel good about it or not. Just get home, find a quiet place, get a notebook and a pen, and write down all the questions you can remember and how you answered them.

It is best not to postpone this task until the following day. Do it as soon as you get home, so it doesn't get messed up in your head. While taking down the notes, analyze your answers, and take note of how you could have answered better. This will help you to be more prepared for your next interview.

Practice and touch on all the topics you covered. Get deep inside knowledge about every one of them. It will help a lot.

When you research all the questions and topics covered, you will have more knowledge about them, and for another interview in the same job profile, you may notice repetitions in the questions asked. This puts you in a better position to answer them. Do not underestimate the power of taking notes.

Bottom line: *Your notebook will help improve your skills for the next interview. Make it a habit to write, analyze, and improve your answers to the questions.*

TIP: DON'T WAIT FOR YOUR INTERVIEW RESULTS.

It doesn't matter if you 'crushed' the interview or feel very good about it, don't just sit around and wait for a call. Instead, you should start preparing for your next interviews.

Whether you feel good about it or not, there is serious uncertainty as to whether you will be accepted. You do not know the exact criteria for recruitments. It may have been on a point you actually missed completely. Also, even if you qualified, what if there were a limited number of candidate openings and the capacity is full? Even if you are accepted, when will they ask you to resume? It can take weeks, months...who knows?

You may have impressed them with your CV and how skilled you were, but what if they didn't like your attitude and used that to shortlist you? What if you waited for months and were not eventually selected? So many 'what ifs'.

So many factors are considered for recruitment, it is hard to determine the outcome. Think again: were you the only candidate for the interview? Can't other people be as intelligent as you are, or maybe even more? Can't they shortlist candidates after they are done with interviews and pick amongst the talented ones? There could have been a thousand reasons why you weren't selected.

Therefore, it is dangerous to relax after an interview.

I have been in contact with several candidates who relaxed after an interview because they felt good about it. They waited 15- 20 days, and yet nothing. They looked all around on social media to see if results had been released, but eventually, they realized they weren't accepted, and they hadn't been preparing for their next interview.

Waiting is very dangerous and it's terrible advice. So why wait? Keep moving, keep going!

Bottom line: Don't wait for the results, tighten your belt for the next interview instead. Put the interview at the back of your mind and move to prepare for future opportunities.

TIP: DO NOT DECIDE FOR YOURSELF THE REASON FOR YOUR REJECTION IF YOU ARE NOT ACCEPTED.

You shouldn't try to figure out the reasons for being rejected. If you do, it should be because you want to go and learn from it.

Some candidates think they have amazing skills but were not selected in the interview because of their poor English speaking or because of less grade if they have.

However, trust me; this doesn't really qualify as a reason for rejection. As long as you have graduated from school, then you have what it takes to present yourself before IT professionals and interviewers.

Even if you were not so fluent in your communication, it doesn't necessarily mean you will be thrown away based on that fact. You can learn these things and the interviewers know this.

Communication and grades are the least important things. Yes, you read it right, the least important things. **Your technical skills are of utmost importance.**

Do you really think that even if you had great communication skills, oral English, and good grades, it is enough to qualify you? No! Your relevant skills to the industry are what matters, and without it, you won't be considered.

More about the communication and low grades fear is addressed in the FEAR REMOVAL section.

Many other candidates believe that they may have done well in the technical interview but lost out in the HR round.

This is laughable because it is the HR professionals who are responsible for the recruitment process. The technical department just carries out interviews on the technical stuff, they aren't actually in charge of rejection or acceptance.

HR considers the results and hires, or rejects based on them. In the end, HR makes the final decision.

In some instances, candidates also say that the interviewers didn't seem knowledgeable and kept asking stupid questions.

Well, in most cases, this is pure arrogance speaking. In a nutshell, you think you are so highly trained and qualified that you are better than your peers. Why else do you think the interviewers asked stupid questions?

This attitude is awful and will affect your performance. Do not ever think this way.

Rather than thinking they are all stupid, realize that every interviewer is different, and work on why you couldn't answer their question or what made you so weak. Try to get better!

FOCUS WORDS

You Are Most Likely To Be Rejected If...

- If you are not able to answer the first few questions in a technical interview.
- If you argue with an interviewer on any question or topic.
- If you are overconfident and show arrogance.

Few focus points...

1. After the technical interview is over, never wait for the result, even if you think that it went excellently. Instead, move on to the next interview, and keep improving your skills; in order to not delay the objective of securing a job. If you are selected, the job offer will come automatically.
2. Keep analyzing what went wrong or if there were any areas or skills for improvement after the technical interview has finished.

FEAR REMOVAL

Tips you'll learn:

- TIP: No room for fear.
- TIP: Don't worry if your communication skills are poor.
- TIP: Don't bother about your low educational marks.
- TIP: Don't think "The IT market is saturated, hence no jobs for me".
- TIP: Don't think that you have to wait for 6 months before re-applying.
- TIP: Don't think that the interview will not be good because you've had no time to refresh your skills.
- TIP: Don't think that you are not well prepared and that attending interviews are a waste of time.

When it comes to written examinations, most fresh graduates are comfortable with it, because it is the form of evaluation they got used to in school. But when it comes to face-to-face interviews, fresh graduates usually fidget and sweat bullets. Their feet begin to get numb; their heart starts to race, and their throat gets dry. Fear and anxiety are always there.

This can be a result of the fact that, as soon as you get invited for a face-to-face interview, your mind fills with doubt, "Will I be able to answer technical questions? Will I get the job?" You might begin to feel underqualified, or you might not trust your communication skills. And it doesn't stop there, you are probably going to look at the other candidates who came for the interview and think about the competition for the job position, wondering whether you stand a chance of being selected. Your mind can raise tons of fear-triggering questions.

Some candidates may be afraid of failing to convey their capabilities and some may worry about their low marks in graduation. They think these issues may cause them to be rejected in interviews and render them unable to get a job.

First of all, it is very common to harbor some fear. What matters is to be able to deal with it and to ensure it does not taint your interview. Fear affects almost every young job seeker in their search for a good position, although some candidates may experience it with more intensity than others.

A most detrimental feeling I have seen a fresh graduate experience is the depression that may result from thinking about the saturation in the IT job market and the fierce competition that arises from it.

I have even come across candidates who do not attend their interviews because of the fear of not being well prepared, even though they are actually skilled in their area of activity.

These fears may have a negative impact on your interview if you are not careful.

This section will help you to determine what kind of fear and anxiety you might be experiencing and will allow you to learn some effective methods to deal with your insecurities and become more confident.

TIP: NO ROOM FOR FEAR.

Believe in yourself. Be confident.!

Fear is not an option, as it plays a detrimental role in deciding the fate of the interview. It is an unnecessary hurdle on your way to securing employment. **Fear will be automatically eradicated when you sharpen and improve your skills**, attaining a level of confidence that will eventually erase any doubts you might have about yourself.

Whenever you attend an interview, you should **see it as an avenue to learn something new**. In almost all cases, during an interview, the selected panel or employer will drop insights on interview techniques, views on the job, as well as other important take-home notes for you. Do not think about a possible positive or negative outcome of the interview. The result will eventually be made known to you.

TIP: DON'T WORRY IF YOUR COMMUNICATION SKILLS ARE POOR.

Many things come under the category of communication; things like whether you can present your ideas effectively, listen properly, how well you can communicate with people, etc. However, in this tip, I **will specifically talk about the English-speaking skill**, that is, oral and written English for non-native speakers.

Many fresh job seekers think they are getting rejected in interviews because they are not fluent in speaking English. Actually, cases like this are really rare, which means you don't have to bother too much. Instead, you need to focus on your skillset.

Here is one real-life experience I want to cite in order to explain why confidence is important regardless of poor communication.

I provided my guidance to a fresh candidate whose English speaking was not good, and he ended up getting his dream job within three months. He does speak in English a little and can at least communicate his knowledge in an interview, though with some grammatical mistakes. Yes, you are reading it right: with grammatical mistakes.

Still, he was the only person that got selected out of 108 candidates after going through a total of 8 rounds of interviews.

Yes, when he had to face the HR stage, HR pointed out his low level of English speaking and said, "*Your English speaking is not so good. Will you work on it to improve?"* He said yes and got an offer letter.

When you are searching for a job, you might not have the time to improve your English speaking. It's not a chapter in a book to finish and automatically start speaking. It needs constant practice and takes a lot of time. So, rather, focus on your skills that will help the organization the most.

However, I would recommend you do cram some sentences that you think can be useful during an interview.

NOTE TO COLLEGE STUDENTS:

If you are still a college student, you obviously have the time to learn, so I would suggest you start working on the oral and written parts of communication in English.

Why is English communication (speaking and writing) important in IT companies, you ask?

Well, generally the spoken language used to communicate in IT companies is English. The local language is also used, but when it comes to discussing projects, tasks, and project issues with your stakeholders (internal clients) and global team across the world, only the English language is effective.

Just think, how would you discuss projects with your team members that include people from countries such as Germany, the USA, etc., or even from other parts of your own country?

English is the only option.

Written English is also important, as you need to write emails, create technical documents, or work with other written material in the company.

And why should a company hire you if your English speaking is poor?

What if you have very strong technical skills, especially ones that are important to a company, but are not good at speaking English? Well, they will hire you, because you will be a valuable resource for their projects. Your team leader can handle the discussions with the global team and others.

NOTE: Ultimately, once you are hired, you have a responsibility to yourself to grow your communication skills.

TIP: DON'T BOTHER ABOUT YOUR LOW EDUCATIONAL MARKS.

Do not worry about your marks if they are low. Instead, focus on improving your skills. Only a few companies have a cut-off for educational marks as a standard procedure; most companies don't.

Some may also consider cut-off marks in walk-ins or as an easy way to shortlist candidates, but the majority of companies look for greatly skilled resources (candidates). So, just focus on skills and move ahead.

I provided my guidance to a candidate who was not getting a job offer and was thinking that his low qualification marks were the reason. *He was thinking that he had attended 6 months of training and was already good at skills and so, he thought that the only reason he wasn't getting any job offers must have been because of his poor marks.*

I asked him to ignore his marks and begin to concentrate his skills in the right direction. I guided him on what to do and in just the next two months, he got a really good job with a good salary in a software company.

By the way, **can you change your marks?** Surely not, so you don't have a choice.

JUST MOVE AHEAD!

Bottom line: *Rather than thinking of marks, move ahead with thorough preparation and your dream job will land at your doorstep for sure.*

TIP: DON'T THINK "THE IT MARKET IS SATURATED, HENCE NO JOBS FOR ME".

"Don't mind competition"

Your focus should be on your job preparation and job search instead of thinking about market saturation or competition. Just think about how you can build your knowledge and stand out in the saturated market.

I have met many technical directors of different companies that say, "*We lack good resources (candidates),*" when in reality, there are tons of resources looking for a job. Aren't these statements contradictory? The technical directors are right in fact.

On this note, I tried guiding candidates and yes, they stand out. One candidate cleared 8 rounds of technical interviews and was selected out of 108 as mentioned earlier, and another candidate stood out from a group of 51.

The golden rule is "*Just focus on building your skills, and there is surely a job for you*".

Never think about market saturation. You will surely get a job.

I understand you may see tons of people struggling for a job in the IT market. You may see tons of people complaining about the competition and market saturation on social media and such. But do you know about them or why they are not getting a job? Look at the positive side instead. Look at the people who are getting their dream jobs and have TOTAL FOCUS on yourself.

When I train my candidates, I ask them not to focus on market saturation but to focus on their skill set. Personally, ***as per observation, I do not find any competition or saturation in the IT market, at least so far.***

TIP: DON'T THINK THAT YOU HAVE TO WAIT FOR 6 MONTHS BEFORE RE-APPLYING.

If you are rejected in an interview in a company, you don't have to wait for the next 6 months to re-apply.

This may be true for a few companies you have to wait but, there are chances that you can attend again and don't have to wait for 6 months.

Many candidates think when they get an interview call from a company, they will prepare well first before applying because of these reasons.

If you don't attend the interview what will happen? You are missing an opportunity even though you are not sure if you will get a chance after 6 months.

This fear will delay your job-hunting process.

Never leave any opportunity!!!

TIP: DON'T THINK THAT THE INTERVIEW WILL NOT BE GOOD BECAUSE YOU'VE HAD NO TIME TO REFRESH YOUR SKILLS.

Sometimes, you may get in situations that won't allow a chance to study for one week or two. And suddenly, you get an opportunity for an interview via may be walk-ins or an arranged interview call or job referral.

Then it comes in your mind that you did not get a chance for revision, and because of that, you feel the interview will not be good, and hence, you don't attend the interview.

Please remove this fear and attend the job interview. You might feel that you forget some things and due to this you might lose confidence but assure yourself that this is not the case, that it is not true.

You shouldn't miss a single opportunity coming your way. **So, don't miss the interview.**

TIP: DON'T THINK THAT YOU ARE NOT WELL PREPARED AND THAT ATTENDING INTERVIEWS ARE A WASTE OF TIME.

The fear of rejection may come to your mind if you think that you are not well prepared.

It has been observed that many candidates do not attend interviews because of this fear. Many of them think that it is a waste of time and money to attend an interview if they feel that they are not well prepared.

To me, I would say this is a big mistake.

Can you measure when you are well prepared? The answer to this question would be difficult.

I'd suggest you attend interviews, even if you think you are not well prepared. Attend interviews regardless and continue with your skill improvements.

You would find the benefits of attending interviews in the Tip: "Attend job interviews even though you are on Training or Self-Study", under the GENERAL tips in the EFFECTIVE INTERVIEW PREPARATION section.

GET ALERT

Tips you'll learn:

- TIP: Beware of fake job calls and emails.
- TIP: Never look for a back-door job.
- TIP: Stick to trying to get a job instead of an internship.

Beware of scammers!

Fresh job candidates, because of their desperation and eagerness to get a job may fall victim to some nefarious people who seek to take advantage of freshers' desperation.

They offer jobs, interviews, and call back under false pretenses for jobs that do not exist.

Usually and from my experience, freshers usually fall for these tricks and end up feeling cheated on and exploited. It may usually lead to depression as they may have lost some money, and all the efforts put into getting that job to become null and void.

This is something that happens very often, and it is only with the right guidance that freshers can protect themselves from it.

Against this backdrop, this topic would reveal some valuable tips on necessary alerts e.g. job traps, fake calls, emails, etc. to ensure you do not fall into these scam traps anymore and waste your hard-earned money and time.

TIP: BEWARE OF FAKE JOB CALLS AND EMAILS.

Job scams are very much real in the recruitment market today, besides the genuine job interviews. You receive fake calls or emails to take a job offer with a very juicy salary package for a really lucrative business.

Do not fall for this scam; it would cost you a huge sum of money. When seeking a job, it is always advisable to look for a security-proof organization to work with. A job search that is safe and fraud-free is highly recommended.

Unfortunately, job scams are very common. It is important that you be in the know about these things and be very aware and alert against fake calls and other job scams. They come in many ways, but to get you started, here is a list of the top signs that indicate job scams and fake calls:

- When recruiters ask you to send your resume to a strange unofficial email.
- When recruiters ask for personal information like bank accounts, addresses, or your card details. Also, if recruiters find your job application on sites and portals, they will have gotten your email as well, so if they ask for that, there is a chance they are scammers. It is important to note that it is common for legitimate recruiters to ask for some of your details, but this happens after the job is offered or awarded, never before!
- When job consultants call you for a job but are unable to disclose their company name, this is usually a sign that they are scammers.

- When recruiters ask to register you or offer you a job but at a financial price or fee. Do not fall for it.

There are other tricks and scam strategies, so it is essential that you are aware of all of them. Be intentional about not falling for them easily or falling at all. It will save you a lot of time, effort, and energy: mental, physical, and otherwise.

Apart from all these, if you can take two major tips to save yourself from job scams, here they are:

1. **IT organizations NEVER ask for money for offering a job**. If they ever ask for money, that means they are fake and just want to scam you. These companies do not take money, rather, they pay you money.
2. Even if you are dealing with IT consultants, they never ask for payment. They are usually being paid by the IT companies themselves, so if they ask for money from you, you are about to be swindled. Don't fall for it.

Never forget the GOLDEN RULE: "Do not pay a single penny to get a job!"

TIP: NEVER LOOK FOR A BACK-DOOR JOB.

Never look for a back-door job!

Now, in case you are wondering what the back door is, it involves paying hefty financial sums to get "in the door" of a company. Whether you pay to get a job, an interview, or just to be selected for an interview, that's taking a back door, and it is not advisable at all. You will not only lose money, but you will also lose other opportunities, mental energy, and maybe even your entire career if you are not careful.

Now, I know what you may be thinking. What if you actually get the job through the back door; what if you're actually employed through the hefty money you paid? Well, believe me, from my experience, even if you don't pay for it now you will eventually pay later. So, it is best and wisest not to do it at all.

You must ask yourself: if you don't have the necessary skills, qualifications, and other requirements, do you think that you can survive for long in the software industry? The short answer is NO! You may be able to get into the company, but you will never last. That is why you should pursue qualifications and skills, rather than going through the back door. A back-door job is just not advisable.

Bottom line: Never go through the back door. Stay away!

TIP: STICK TO TRYING TO GET A JOB INSTEAD OF AN INTERNSHIP.

It is recommended that you stick to your initial goal of getting a full-time job rather than just an internship.

Later on, I will address internships, what they are, and my real- time experiences with them.

In the meantime, know that most companies offer internships spanning between 3-6 months. They may even ask you to do a 6-month internship for free. They will tell you that by doing so, you'll gain knowledge and have maximum exposure to the industry, after which you will be given a permanent position.

It is important to note that an internship is not a guarantee for a job!

At the end of the day, it all boils down to what you want. If you want to accept an internship or go with your dream job, the choice is yours.

But be extremely certain that you give good thought to the uncertainty of getting a permanent position, and to the 6 months of your valuable time that you'll spend there.

After considering these factors, you can go ahead and make your decision.

However, while advising my previous candidates and mentees, I've never really recommended pursuing an internship program. Rather, I encourage chasing down your dream job.

Is there such a thing as a good internship?

Yes, actually. In some instances, it is wise to accept an internship position. Some big firms offer internships for up to 3 months and ensure they teach you a lot and show you the ropes of the industry. They give you maximum exposure, and after 3 months, you'll have gained plentiful knowledge and skills to make you more competitive in job hunting.

Also, some of these firms offer internships as a test or recruitment process. To be recruited, you may have to go through their internship program and be trained in their methods. That way, you will be a perfect staff member at their firm.

But as you can imagine, and as earlier stated, there is no guarantee that the firm you are targeting is like this. For this reason, I personally don't recommend internships, but once again, it is all up to you!

Here are some real-life instances of the uncertainty of internships:

Once, in one of the software companies where I worked, many fresh graduates joined on a one-year internship basis in the hopes of retaining a job at the firm. After one year, all of them were not retained and had to struggle to go look for a job elsewhere. It must have been so devastating to them.

On the other hand, another of my trainees, after taking some of my training, decided to go for a 3-month internship (with handsome pay) with a certain firm. After the 3 months, he didn't get a permanent job, but he gained a lot of skills and experiences in the end. So you see, he did not waste his time at all.

However, there was also another instance of another candidate and trainee of mine. He decided to opt into a company's internship program without pay, thinking he would get a permanent job with them. From my experience, I knew this wouldn't be the case, so I advised him not to go.

He didn't listen and went on anyway. It took this candidate a month for him to realize he was on the wrong path, and to see the reality that he was wasting his time and not really gaining much skill. He finally decided to take my advice and opted out of the internship program.

When he did, he continued his job-hunting and within a month, he bagged a permanent job. See my point?

FOCUS WORDS

1. Do not go to an interview worried or afraid. Do not stress about securing that particular job or else you will lose focus and become demotivated, which will negatively impact your performance in the interviews. Rather, attend interviews to learn from your mistakes and improve your skills. Job offers will come automatically if you are selected.
2. When job hunting, do not be deterred if you don't meet the educational requirements or if there is a great deal of market competition. Focus on improving your skills set, instead. Most of the employers want their job done and you can do it. There is no place for fear while job hunting.
3. IT organizations NEVER ask for money for offering a job.

EFFECTIVE INTERVIEW PREPARATION

In this section, you will find tips and strategies on effective ways to prepare for an IT job interview i.e. written test, technical and HR., brief of the recruitment process, and much more. You will learn what employers look for in a fresh graduate, which will push you in the right direction towards preparing you for the job you desire. You will also receive general tips and highlights that will allow you to stand out from the crowd; something that is vital in order to gain your dream job.

The majority of fresh graduates put in all the hard work, immerse themselves in loads of topics on various technologies and languages, take on extra training to ensure they can crack an interview, but ultimately fail due to a lack of right direction and not knowing the right strategies for job preparation.

Many freshers and already trained candidates that have been looking for a job for months come to me in frustration explaining that they are just not getting a job in the IT industry and can't understand why. When I talk to them and conduct mock interviews, they are able to see for themselves that they were lacking the right strategies for job preparation.

So, in this book, you will discover the right direction towards learning the practical tips and strategies to prepare for your job interviews. But before moving further, I would like to briefly discuss the insights of recruitment processes in an IT company for fresh graduates. This will give you an idea of different types of interviews conducted by the companies and how and why they get conducted.

Recruitment Process Insights

You may be familiar with the fact that during a recruitment process in the software industry, a written test, technical interview, and an HR interview are conducted for a fresh candidate. But I want to give you some more insight into the process to help you gain a better understanding.

Written Test

The first step of the recruitment process is the written test. Typically, the written test is also termed as the screening test. It is carried out by the companies to shortlist candidates because it would be very difficult for recruiters to provide the technical test for all of the candidates. You should be aware that hundreds of fresh candidates may attend the job walk-ins, off-campus or on-campus placements. So, the written test is primarily conducted for shortlisting the candidates.

It is also observed that some companies do not take a written test. What they do instead is conduct a technical interview directly if the number of candidates is under a certain number, for example at least less than 50.

A fresher could also be shortlisted via telephone for an interview and called for technical and HR interviews in person, but the chances are very low.

A written test can be conducted offline or online.

Written test patterns vary from company to company as the examples shown below:

Pattern-1: Objectives questions on the quantitative aptitude, Logical and verbal reasoning, and puzzle, and so on.

Pattern-2: Objectives questions on the quantitative aptitude, logical reasoning, with the objectives on some technical subjects such as C, C++, OS, Java, SQL, Linux. depending upon the company's job requirements.

Pattern-3: Aptitude and coding problems and so on.

Pattern-4: You may be given a list of coding problems that you have to write their solutions on a paper, board, or computer.

There can be multiple patterns for the written test, but mostly it will include topics from the above-mentioned patterns.

Technical Interview

A technical interview is conducted to determine whether you are suitable for the job or not, whether you will be able to write code for the company's project, or if you would be able to understand codes and so on. In the technical interviews, recruiters check your coding skills, algorithms, problem-solving skills, and technical knowledge in the related fields such as Java, C++, Python, and Testing, etc. It also assesses soft skills such as communication, learning attitude, and so on.

Multiple rounds of technical interviews can also be conducted, but the number of technical rounds varies from company to company.

In the technical interviews, you could be asked about technical concepts from topics that you have specified in your resume. Coding problems can also be given to be solved. In addition, some puzzles can also be asked but this is not guaranteed.

Hr Interview

In brief, the HR (Human Resource) of a company is responsible for recruiting candidates, overseeing payroll, assisting employees, and arranging training, etc.

Generally, during the recruitment process, the HR finds, screens, and shortlists candidates for an interview and forwards the information on to the technical panels. Depending on the result of the technical panel, HR then holds an interview to discuss formalities, processes, and salaries. But before this stage, HR may ask you some questions to find out more about your personality. This is done mainly to see if you are an all-round good match for the company, even if you are technically strong. You will be provided with tips on HR and interview question guidelines in the upcoming section.

WRITTEN

Generally, final year students start preparing for written skills test when their on-campus placement is near, and fresh graduates do it when they begin to search for an off-campus job. You probably won't have much time to prepare for it, because, in addition to preparing for the written test, you must study technical subjects such as the programming language, coding problems, algorithms, and so forth. Honestly, that is a challenge in itself.

If you have been honing your abilities for the aptitude, logical, and oral tests for a long time, you are at an advantage. But what if you have not had enough time to get ready? Then you are going to need a strategic plan to prepare for the written test, and in the coming tips, I am going to explain how to do it.

Tips you'll learn:

- TIP: Choose the strategy that best suits you when preparing for the written test.
- TIP: Do not focus on aptitude, logic, and verbal ability in episodes; rather, be regular and spend less time on them in general.
- TIP: Gather all the important formulas for quantitative aptitude and logical questions.
- TIP: Focus on fundamental concepts to solve objective technical questions.

TIP: CHOOSE THE STRATEGY THAT BEST SUITS YOU WHEN PREPARING FOR THE WRITTEN TEST.

Here I will tell you some strategies for the written interview test preparation. These are purely based on observation. You must choose the strategies that are most suitable for you and work on them.

Strategy-1: Aptitude + logical reasoning + verbal ability + technical MCQs + coding problems + data structure and algorithms + Group Discussion (30% chance to be asked)
Strategy-2: Aptitude + logical reasoning + verbal ability + coding problems + data structure and algorithms.
Strategy-3: Aptitude + logical reasoning+ coding problems + data structure and algorithms.
Strategy-4: Coding problems + data structure and algorithms.

Strategies 1 and 2 are the best fit for final year students for on-campus placement or students who want to prepare for jobs before reaching the final year. I also recommend going with strategy 1 if time allows you.

Strategies 2, 3, and 4 are the best fit for off-campus interviews because fresh graduates do not get a lot of time to prepare for the written test while searching for jobs in the market.

Most of my off-campus candidates adopted strategy 3, which worked well for them and helped them get their dream job.

It should be noted that as you move down choosing a strategy from the list, the degree of chances of opportunities in some interviews will decrease and you will also be rejected in some screening rounds. Choose them carefully, considering the time and effort that you will be able to make.

What if you really do not have time to prepare for the written test, and still want to get your dream job?

Consider strategy 4. Though it is less recommended because of the probability of losing some job opportunities, it also works.

What will happen if you do not focus on aptitude, logical reasoning, verbal ability, or GD? Well, you may be rejected in the screening test and you may lose specific job opportunities. It does not matter how excellently you are prepared for technical skills.

But there is also a chance that some companies will only ask coding problems in the written test. You can be rejected in 6 out of 10 companies because you did not prepare in aptitude, logical reasoning, etc., but think of the 4 interviews where only coding problems are asked. Since you have already spent a huge amount of time focusing on and improving your technical skills instead of the rest, one of those interviews must be yours, so crack it.

For my candidates who were just average in aptitude and reasoning, I asked them to get an extra level of knowledge in technical skills. They faced companies who asked aptitude and logic questions in the written test, and they failed. They simply ignored it. But when they got a chance where only technical skills were required, **they cracked it.**

TIP: DO NOT FOCUS ON APTITUDE, LOGIC, AND VERBAL ABILITY IN EPISODES; RATHER, BE REGULAR AND SPEND LESS TIME ON THEM IN GENERAL.

It has been observed that people start preparing for the quantitative aptitude, logical and verbal questions in episodes. This means that they stop working on technical subjects such as programming and coding for periods of time, in order to focus on aptitudes, logic, and verbal subjects instead.

Do not make this mistake. Rather, study these topics regularly, but spend less time on them. Focus on and give more attention to improving your technical skills.

Prepare for aptitude and logical reasoning and so on, but do not give too much priority to it and be regular. Generally, as per observation, the written test is taken to shortlist candidates. Some companies may have these tests in the process but not all companies do. Thus, your technical skills matter the most and you should focus on these skills.

You know very well how much time aptitude and GD preparation takes and how challenging it is. You can save a lot of time by putting a smaller effort into aptitudes preparation and use that time to master your technical skills. ***You must give only a little effort to aptitudes, logical and verbal ability, etc. and spend way more time preparing your technical skills.***

TIP: GATHER ALL THE IMPORTANT FORMULAS FOR QUANTITATIVE APTITUDE AND LOGICAL QUESTIONS.

Do you have time to practice thousands of problems on aptitude and logical available over the internet and in the books during your job hunt and preparation for a written interview test in the software industry?

You know well that you cannot read all of them. You need the right method of preparing for aptitude and logical problems.

My strategy is, *I would not say that you should practice as many questions as you can, but instead, you should set a defined limit over them, so you can finish in a specified time.*

Here are ways you can set a limit over them and finish quickly. Believe me, it works.

1. Choose topics, understand the concepts well,
2. Write down all the related formulas and tricks with an example. In fact, create notes on it.
3. Practice 2 to 3 problems on each formula and tricks to get confidence on the topic.

Here is a concrete example:

Choose a topic, speed, and distance. Understand the concept, write all the formulas and tricks with an example in notes, practice a few problems on all the formulas and tricks.

For the first time, creating notes requires effort, but it would be a fantastic tool for revision in futures to come.

TIP: FOCUS ON FUNDAMENTAL CONCEPTS TO SOLVE OBJECTIVE TECHNICAL QUESTIONS.

Work on the fundamental knowledge of topics such as C, C++, Java, data structures and algorithms, OS, SQL, and Linux, etc. that should be sufficient to solve the Objective (multiple choice questions) questions for the written interview test.

The important point is that to increase your confidence level, you can practice some multiple-choice questions, but do not dedicate too much time to it. You can find tons of objective questions on related topics over the internet to practice.

Generally, the objective questions for the written test are built on the fundamentals of these topics. Some questions may be asked on programming and output. This means, a small piece of code will be given, and you will need to tell the correct output. If your fundamentals are clear and you have practiced some programming, it should not be difficult for you.

Just for your information, the technical objective questions may not contain all the topics mentioned above and not all the companies include technical objective questions in their written interview test.

TECHNICAL

In this section, you are going to learn some powerful and effective ways to prepare for technical interviews. It will help you learn what subjects are important and should be prioritized in order to effectively reduce your overload of study, allowing you to prepare yourself for an interview in less time. In addition, you are going to learn the right way to prepare for technical interviews if you have a specific area of interest or job profile.

Tips you'll learn:

- TIP: Choose one Object-Oriented programming language and master It.
- TIP: Focus on coding problems practice.
- TIP: Practice coding problems and data structure and algorithms in the right way.
- TIP: Have a good hold on Database basics
- TIP: Spice up the core topics.
- TIP: If you are drawn to a specific area for your first job, go about it in the right way.
- TIP: Find the fastest way to improve your skills in your subjects.

TIP: CHOOSE ONE OBJECT-ORIENTED PROGRAMMING LANGUAGE AND MASTER IT.

During your graduation, you study multiple programming languages such as C and object-oriented programming languages like C++, Java, C#, and Python, etc. Many fresh graduates try to master all the languages they were taught during college to prepare for on-campus or off-campus placement interviews. However, it may be very difficult to master every language at the fresher level and you may not have time to master them all during your job hunt. So, aiming to master all of the languages would not be efficient or the best way to prepare for your job interview.

I would recommend, rather than trying to learn every programming language, picking one object-oriented language and mastering it. **Get a deeper level of knowledge about it and practice well.** *In the coming tips, I will tell you what level of OOP concepts to learn for an impressive interview performance that will make you stand out from the crowd, and how you can achieve this quickly.*

Choosing one programming language gives you the following benefits.

1) You stop switching language to solve coding problems.

The major problem I have seen in a fresh graduate is that when he solves a coding problem, he tries to switch from one language to another. For example, sometimes he uses C/C++ language and sometimes Java, etc. Believe me, it is not effective from the interview perspective. So, you should choose one language to solve coding problems. Switching languages to solve coding problems will waste your time and make you inefficient, which is not what you want during your job hunt.

2) You get strong concepts and hold on code syntax.

In a technical interview, the programming concepts or a piece of codes are asked so that the interviewer can understand how efficient you are in a programming language.

If you have chosen one programming language and practice regularly, then you will obviously demonstrate good command over the concepts, code syntax, complex code understanding, and writing and the readymade libraries available for the data structures and algorithms to solve coding problems.

Recommendation:

As per observation, most fresh graduate writes multiple programming languages in their resume such as "C, C++, Java" or "C, C++, C#" or "C, C++, Python" etc. as they have studied all in the graduation. I would suggest highlighting **one programming language on which you are strong, or you have decided to master**, in the summary section of the resume. For the rest programming language mention that you have a basic knowledge.

TIP: FOCUS ON CODING PROBLEMS PRACTICE.

You need to keep the focus on coding skills and practice it regularly. Almost every company is in search of a candidate that is good at coding, problem-solving techniques, and data structure and algorithms. Recruiters check your capability and how good you are at solving a problem by effectively utilizing data structures and algorithms.

Here are some examples of coding problems to give you an idea. In the next tip, you will get to understand the right strategies to work on this for more effective and quicker job preparation.

- What is the sum of the integer array elements?
- Find the missing number between 0-100 in an array.
- Find the smallest and highest elements of an integer array.
- Check if a string is a palindrome etc.
- Check if a tree is a BST (Binary Search Tree)
- Find a factorial of a number using recursion.
- Remove duplicates in an integer array.
- Reverse a given string etc.

To solve coding problems, you need to be good at data structures and algorithms. And, you need to be capable of choosing the right data structures and algorithms to solve them.

Here Are Some Examples Of Data Structures And Algorithms:

Data structures: Array, Linked list, Stack, Queue, Hash map, trees, Binary Search Tree and Graph, etc.

Algorithms: Bubble sort, quick sort, insertion sort, and bucket sort, binary search, breadth-first search, and depth-first search, etc.

Get A Sense Of Time Complexity And Space Complexity:

You also need to have a reasonable sense of time complexity and space complexity of algorithms to write efficient code for a better performance of an application.

In brief, Time Complexity: Amount of time taken by an algorithm to run for a set of input data.

Space Complexity: It is the amount of memory space taken by an algorithm to run for a set of input data.

You need to understand **Big O notation** to represent complexities.

For example, the Big O notation for bubble sort algorithms is O(n2) and for the quicksort is O (n log n). The bubble sort performance is good for a smaller set of data and the quick sort is good for a larger set of data inputs and so on.

NOTE

1. Practicing coding problems will **help in both written and technical interviews.** In the coding rounds, you will be given problems to solve on a piece of paper or directly on a computer or an online platform, and you need to write the solution and code for them.
2. **Every day** you should solve and practice at least two coding problems. If you find some of the coding problems difficult, then solve and practice them repeatedly. It should be a daily routine.

ALERT:

Some fresh graduates who look for a job off-campus in the market, choose for the testing job profile and get the impression that they don't need to practice coding problems as it is not required for the testing job. I will recommend coming out of this impression and putting it into practice.

TIP: PRACTICE CODING PROBLEMS AND DATA STRUCTURE AND ALGORITHMS IN THE RIGHT WAY.

Here I'll tell you the right and effective strategies to practice coding problems and learn data structures and algorithms. It will really help you get prepared in an effective and faster way. Trust me, it works well.

1. Start Solving coding problems and learn the data structures and algorithms on the fly:

   Do not try to learn all the data structures and algorithms first, and then start solving coding problems. Rather, start picking coding problems and learn the data structure and algorithms as you go.

   For example, if you pick a coding problem like "*sort the elements of an integer array containing 20 elements*".

   Then, you can learn about the *array* data structure thoroughly and *bubble sort* or *insertion sort* algorithms, etc to solve it.

   Consider another problem, "Check if a tree is a BST". Learn about the binary search tree and then solve this problem.

   What if you do not get a clue about a data structure or algorithm by reading the coding question?

   For the previous two examples, you get clues about the data structure i.e. you need to learn the *array* and *BST*. **But what if you do not get any clue?**

Consider a coding problem, *"Store id and name of 10 students in a data structure and find their name by id"*.

In this case, if you don't get an idea about what data structure to use to solve this problem, then, search the solution on google first, if you still don't get an idea, then ask people on a social media group and you will get the idea. So, let us say you got an idea that a key-value pair can be maintained in a Hash Map data structure, then, you learn about the *hash map* and operations performed on it and then solve the problem.

2. Start Learning Data Structures and Algorithms in 2 Phases:

First phase:

The first phase is easier to grab and get you enough confidence to solve coding problems. These data structures and algorithms help solve most of the coding problems asked the fresh graduates.

Data structures: Array, Linked list, Stack, Queue, Hash map, basic of the tree, and Binary Search Tree.

Algorithms: Bubble sort, quick sort, insertion sort, and bucket sort, binary search, and recursion.

Second phase:

If you feel that you have good commands over the items mentioned in the first phase and you have sufficient time during your job hunt, you can move to the second phase.

Data structures: Advanced trees such as AVL Tree and other types of trees and Graph etc.

Algorithms: Breadth-first search and depth-first search, finding patterns and others, etc.

3. Do Not Just Read, Understand, and Copy Paste Solutions to the Coding Problems:

   You get a list of coding problems and their solutions on multiple resources i.e. YouTube, Website, Book or pdf, etc. How do you learn and practice them?

   How most people practice a coding problem?

   They pick a coding problem e.g. "*check if a number is odd or even*" and jump straight to the solution. Either they just understand it by reading it or copy-paste the code in their compiler, compile and run. That's it and Done.

   This is not an effective way to learn and practice. Initially, I was also doing the same. But by the time, I analyzed that I was doing it in the wrong way. Because, after some time I used to forget or if the same problem was asked again after some time in an interview, I was doing mistakes. In the worst case, when an interviewer used to tweak the coding problems, there was a complete blank or stuck happening.

   In the bottom line, by just reading and understanding the solution of the problem, and practice by copy and paste, do not get you much capability to solve a new coding problem.

What is the right way to practice a coding problem?

First, try yourself.

Here are the effective steps to learn and practice.

- Pick a coding problem.
- Write your logic for the complete solution.
- Write the code for the logic on a paper.
- Write the code on a computer, compile, and run it.

If still, you are not able to get to the solution.

Look at the given solutions on the resources such as websites, YouTube, etc. and follow the steps.

- Understand the logic and then the solution's code.
- If the solution does not contain logic but only code, then understand the code and write the logic on a paper.
- Write the code on paper.
- Manually write the code on your computer, compile and run it. **No copy-pastes!**

NOTE:

1. You don't have to solely focused on solving as many problems as you can by just understanding and copy-pasting the code. Because it will not build a strong foundation. It will just give you the impression that you practiced coding problems a lot and you get satisfaction. But the ground reality will be different.
2. In fact, you need the ability to code fast and accurately. You need to get the capability to solve the new and unseen problems. So, you should follow the correct method to practice.
3. Try to use the readymade library for data structures and algorithms to solve a coding problem instead of your own version.

   When you solve a coding question, and if a data structure or an algorithm is required, use the already well-written data structures and algorithms from the available library for respective programming languages.

   For example,

   Java programming language users can use the java collection package to use already inbuilt data structures and algorithms. C++ users can use STL and so on.

It has been observed that the few candidates start writing their own version of the data structure to solve a problem. It is time-consuming and is not required.

Keep in mind that interviewers want to know how you can effectively utilize data structures or algorithms to solve a given problem. They are not interested in your own version of data structures and algorithms.

However, sometimes they may specifically ask to implement your own version. For example, implement a *linked list* or *strlen* function to get the length of a string, etc.

In simple words, to solve a coding problem you should use data structure and algorithms from the inbuilt library unless it is specified to implement your own version.

4. Act and start practicing it immediately. **Pick twenty-five** coding problems to kick start and see the difference in your confidence. You can find the fine blended list of coding problems on my website (Visit FAQ and study resources section of this book).

   You don't need to solve an unlimited number of coding problems at the fresher level. Reach the target of practicing fifty coding problems and your confidence will tell you if you need to practice more.

TIP: HAVE A GOOD HOLD ON DATABASE BASICS

Learn the SQL (Structured Query Language) language that is used in a database such as SQL Server, MySQL, and Oracle, etc. You can choose any one of the databases to practice.

Note that the SQL is not asked in every company but the companies who work on the database. **But still, I would recommend** learning the basics as learning the basics is easy and quick. Moreover, to have more job opportunities as a fresher.

You might be familiar with the SQL database topics; however, I would like to list down some topics for your convenience and to keep focus to learn them fast. Make sure you are just not reading about them but practicing them and creating notes while you study them. If you learn and practice these topics, you would also be able to write the basic SQL queries that are asked in an interview.

Here is the SQL database topics list:

Database: create, drop

Table: Create, drop, insert, update, select, delete, alias, re-name, and truncate.

Constraints: Not, Null, Unique, Default, Check Primary Key, and Foreign Key

Altering table: add a column, drop a column, and rename a column.

Aggregate functions: Count, Max, Min, Sum, and Average, etc.

SQL statements: Distinct, Order by, Group by, Where, Having, Logical Operators – AND, OR and NOT, IN, NOT IN, BETWEEN.,

EXISTS AND NOT EXISTS, LIKE AND WILD CARDS, SQL SUBQUERY, SELECT INTO.

Difference Between SQL statements: Where Vs Having, Primary key Vs Unique Key, Function Vs Stored Procedure, Delete Vs Truncate Vs Drop, Union Vs Union All.

Commands: DDL, DML, TCL, DCL

ACID properties, 1 NF (normal form), 2 NF, 3NF

Joins: Inner, Left, Right, Full and Self Join

The mentioned list above should be on priority. If you have time in your hands, you can go with topics such as views, triggers, etc. and more as per your interest.

TIP: SPICE UP THE CORE TOPICS.

This tip will show you how to spice up the core topics (***One programming language** of your choice with a deeper level of knowledge and **strong coding problems***) with basic knowledge of other topics. But, first let me give you a little insight into the industry's hiring process, to give you a more comprehensive understanding and help you choose topics effectively to spice up the core topics.

IT companies will primarily look for fresh graduates to fulfill the role of developers and Tester profiles, in their respective domains, such as web development, mobile, windows applications, etc. But most companies test fresh graduates on the core topics before they hire candidates for their desired roles and profiles.

Furthermore, as an example, you may get a job as a java developer - at the fresher level; but once you have joined the company, you could then be assigned to a python project or Testing or web development, depending upon the company's requirements. One of my candidates aced the interview for a java profile role but was then assigned for work on python web development. It all depends on the company's requirements.

Mastering the core topics is an invaluable tool when it comes to job interviews. In fact, in my experience, all the candidates who had exceptional performance and knowledge of these topics quickly acquired their first job. However, I would recommend that in addition to the core topics, you also add other related topics with the basic knowledge for your desired role within the company, due to the following benefits:

- When recruiters search for potential candidates, who match their desired profile on job portals, they use these different topics as part of their search and the job portal will reveal your resume to them.
- Secondly, a company that is looking for a specific profile will have a little more confidence in your abilities.

Below, I give you some examples of what I mean by extending the core topics with other topics with just basic knowledge for your desired profiles.

Web Development Profile:

For web development, you can add HTML, CSS, and JavaScript, etc. You can add a related framework name as well. For example, if you choose the core topic as Python, then you can add the Django framework.

Testing Profile:

You can add SDLC, manual, and automation testing and get the idea of defect management systems such as JIRA and HPQC, etc.

Java Developer Profile:

You can add topics such as hibernate and spring framework etc.

C# Developer Profile:

You can add topics such as WPF and WCF etc.

Here is one sample including core topics:

- C# & OOPs – strong
- Coding problems - strong
- SQL – Basics
- WPF – Medium level at least
- WCF- Just a basic idea.

Similarly, you can compile topics for the desired job profile you have chosen.

NOTE

1. You only need to know the basics of the supplementary topics. You should remain focused on the core topics and make them super strong.
2. Spice up the core topics with others but be careful not to overload yourself.

Warning: do not overwhelm your resume with other topics that you are not knowledgeable in, simply in response to the resume exposer or to impress the recruiters. If you cannot answer basic questions about the other topics it will impact your technical interview negatively.

Attention: If your on-campus placement is far away or the time allows you, then you are not limited to extend your knowledge in the supplementary topics at a deeper level besides the core topics.

TIP: IF YOU ARE DRAWN TO A SPECIFIC AREA FOR YOUR FIRST JOB, GO ABOUT IT IN THE RIGHT WAY.

The same subjects are taught to all graduates in college, but some graduates find themselves pulled to a specific area, such as: data science, Big data, and IoT, etc. Mostly, they are drawn to this specific area due to their interest, or they are post-graduate in that area or think that they will secure a job faster due to less competition.

Note that if you are choosing only a specific domain to get your first job, you are narrowing down the scope of potential job opportunities. As, generally, companies look for experienced candidates in these areas, due to their cost and the timeline required to build a project.

Am I trying to demotivate you? No, not at all.

My point is, that with this mindset, your job opportunities will be reduced, and you may get fewer interview calls. It is definitely possible for you to secure a job in these areas, but you must be exceptionally skilled, as well as have some applications or projects to showcase as a piece of evidence. Note, that doing the specific certifications can help a little; however, it does not give interviewers much confidence.

So, I would like to recommend to you the right strategy for trying to secure your first job in a specific area.

You should keep preparing and attending interviews in your specific area of interest but also focus on the topics i.e. one object-oriented programming language of your choice with deeper level knowledge, practice coding problems, and basics of SQL.

Oftentimes when fresh graduates focus on a specific area, they neglect to focus on the core topics which have been mentioned here.

TIP: FIND THE FASTEST WAY TO IMPROVE YOUR SKILLS IN YOUR SUBJECTS.

Now, you might have decided what skills and topics you need to prepare for your job interviews. Your goal of focussing on which topics to concentrate on is now clear.

You must now focus on how fast you can prepare specific topics. If your on-campus placement is near or you are already looking for a job off-campus, then you may not have much time for your job preparation. You should find a way to prepare your subjects as fast as possible.

The ideal time for the job interview preparation should be approx. 2-3 months. This is definitely possible as per experiments and observations on my candidates demonstrate.

You should now know better how to prepare your topics fast. But in terms of time, here are some resources that can help you upskill your topics at a faster rate:

- YouTube is your best friend. However, you can find short duration courses online for the topics you have selected.
- Find a software professional online who can teach you the subject in the shortest time. You can enquire on social media platforms or somewhere off-line or online if anybody can teach you.
- Find a workshop in a training institute (online or offline). Workshops are of shortest periods (2-7 days).

During the introductory portion of the heading "*Effective Interview Preparation*", you have already read the role of HR during the recruitment process. Here, you will get tips and guidelines on how to respond acceptably to some tricky and misleading HR interview questions. Also, many fresh graduates have the false impression that they have been rejected in the HR round, despite having done well in the technical interview. In reality, it might not have been so. You will get a clear picture of it so that you can proceed with your job preparation in the right direction.

Tips you'll learn:

- TIP: Kill the thought of rejection in the HR Round.
- TIP: Prepare your answers to these few HR Questions prior to interviews.

TIP: KILL THE THOUGHT OF REJECTION IN THE HR ROUND.

I have come across several candidates who feel they messed up in the HR round even though they have good skills and are technically sound. Because of this, they no more focus on their skills anymore but wait for job interview calls only.

I had a few candidates who felt this way, they felt they were eliminated in the HR round, but their technical skills are sound.

So, I decided to get to the bottom of this by conducting a mock interview. In the end, we realized that their technical skills were not as good as they thought.

Also, once again, you must realize that the HR teams do not recruit in isolation, they use the results given to them by the technical interviewers, so if you performed very well at the technical stage, you may be hired.

The HR acts on information by the technical department, they then conduct an interview to see if you should be hired.

The technical department does not give feedback to you, it is only the HR that does, and this then gives the impression that they make the final decision. Please do not be deceived, pay that thought no mind.

So, you should focus on improving your technical skills without thinking that you are getting rejected in an HR interview. There is a rare chance that you will get rejected in the HR round.

TIP: PREPARE YOUR ANSWERS TO THESE FEW HR QUESTIONS PRIOR TO INTERVIEWS.

In my opinion, you should not burn too much of your time over HR interview preparation. Focus instead on your skillset.

It is difficult to say exactly what questions HR is going to ask, but it should not be very difficult for you to answer. **Just be polite, honest, and practical. That's it, you're good to go**. You will be able to answer well.

However, I would like to offer a few frequently asked questions to give you an idea about what the HR interview may entail.

It should be noted that these questions **can be asked by the technical panel or even the manager.**

Whatever I feel are tricky and important HR questions and guidelines are what I'm including here. I believe you can answer the rest easily. If you are curious about more questions, you can Google and get an idea, **but please do not burn much time on it. Instead, focus on your subject's preparation.**

Also, you should know how you are going to answer these types of questions before an interview. I would recommend that you compose your answers ahead of time, write them down on paper, and practice speaking them.

Questions & Answers with Guidelines

1) Tell me about yourself?

Read the answer in the "*During A Technical Interview*" section.

2) Do you have any questions for me?

Read the answer in the "*During A Technical Interview*" section.

3) What are your strengths and weaknesses?

For this question, I would like to give you some guidelines with examples, so you can prepare your effective answer accordingly.

Generally, it is easy to tell the strengths. But, telling the weakness is a very difficult part of preparing your strengths and weaknesses. Don't worry I will make it simple for you with this tip.

When this question is asked, we quickly and happily tell the strength but just as quickly get stuck at weakness.

Many candidates think that if we accept, we have weaknesses, then we can be rejected.

Even I was also not able to answer this question properly, even after 4 years of experience. I was also thinking that my weakness can be the cause of my rejection.

But, after I discussed this topic with some senior company associates and a technical manager, it was only then I realized the truth.

Telling and knowing your weakness is not bad but rather good and this can never be the cause of rejection. Interestingly, it will impress the interviewer that you can accept your weakness/ mistakes.

It is important to note that, whenever you are telling your weakness, **never forget to include how you are going to improve it.**

By the way, nobody is perfect in this world and everyone has weaknesses. This is 100% truth, if we don't accept our weakness then we will never improve it.

I would like to help you write your weaknesses in an impressive format you can happily tell in interviews.

First of all, write a list of your strength and weakness on paper. Select one or two weakness that is related to jobs or organization.

Here are some examples of weakness,

Example-1:

I have poor communication skills. I am trying to improve on it. I am following books and/or websites (*tell the name of books and websites whatever you follow*)

It is better to write down those books or websites or both, so you don't forget to tell them the name. Remember, referencing whatever you are following helps build trust.

Example-2:

I am a very reserved person and don't talk much to people. I am trying to make an improvement on it, so in this organization, I can communicate with my team effectively.

Example-3:

I am poor and lazy at writing documents. For example, I might have written the code but if you ask me to write a flow chart or about the code, I get bored writing documents. To make improvements on it I have started writing about codes or what algorithms I learn and try to write about it in doc or pdf format.

There can be many weaknesses in your related field. Just compose your strength and weakness and you will find how easy it is.

Q) How long would you work here if we hire you?

You should honestly answer this question. Some people answer that they will stay forever or for many years in the company just to get the job. Think about yourself if this is true. Are you really going to stay forever?

You can rather answer in the following way.

Answer: I will stay here as long as I see career growth (Learning + work + salary) and have a good relationship with the organization.

Q) Can you work extra hours, late-night, or on weekends?

Just for the sake of getting a job do not answer simply YES. It is better to show the responsibilities and answer practically.

Answer: I would not like to work on weekends or late hours, but if the urgency arises, maybe in project delivery to meet deadlines, then surely, I will stretch myself to late hours or for the sake of task completion. But this cannot be a daily routine.

I need weekends holiday to relax, spend time with my family. Or I may have some personal work to complete, skills to update, training, etc.

It is all about work-life balance, which is important to be productive in an organization.

Q) What are your salary expectations?

Generally, at a fresh graduate's level, most companies have a standard salary structure. However, they may ask if you have a particular figure in your mind. Accordingly, they may adjust the salary in some form if they wish to or sometimes that may depend upon some factors.

Recommend telling your reasonable figure with some valid reasons, for example, "*this is a costly city*", or "*you are paying a loan for your education*". Do not bother if you are going to get it or not. HR will investigate it and act accordingly.

NOTE: There is no issue in negotiating for salary as a fresh graduate with valid reasons.

Q) You are very talented. Would you like to work as an individual on a project or with a team?

Generally, this question is asked to check if you have a mindset of working with a team and in a collaborative environment.

Answer: I can work as an individual but will prefer working with the team. Because I strongly believe that a team produces great results.

FOCUS WORDS

What Does an Employer Really Look for In A Fresh Graduate?

Employers look for fresh candidates who can independently solve problems in their respective domains, write quality code, understand the project and its existing code quickly, do quality testing of their product, communicate to the team and work in a collaborative environment, etc.

- Without much supervision, you should be able to understand and comprehend a company's project. To do this, you need to have very good technical skills.
- Attitude and willingness to learn. These assets are needed when a company is looking to hire for projects which will require different technologies, programming languages, and platforms. If you have a positive attitude and a willingness to learn, it helps the projects to run more smoothly.

So, recruiters primarily look for candidates who have strong coding skills, knowledge of algorithms, and a master of any one language that shows your capability.

STAND OUT FROM THE CROWD

The tips and guidelines that you have studied so far already make you exceptional and different from the others. However, in this section, you are going to learn what can make you stand out even more. In fact, as per my experience, these tips will make you ridiculously stand out from the crowd. These tips are not expected to be known by a fresh graduate so, if you follow this and act on it, it will make you rise above the competition.

Tips you'll learn:

- TIP: Take the Object-Oriented Programming Concepts to the next level.
- TIP: Showcase your Skills and Work Samples online.
- TIP: Write code with comments and meaningful names of variables and functions.
- TIP: Mention in your resume's summary that you're familiar with the object-oriented design principles and design patterns.

TIP: TAKE THE OBJECT-ORIENTED PROGRAMMING CONCEPTS TO THE NEXT LEVEL.

Taking the oops concepts to the next level is one of the major reasons to make you stand out from the crowd in a technical interview. Because it is very difficult to achieve this level of concepts for majority of the fresh graduates.

By following these guidelines, you will distinguish yourself from the competition and make your interview impressive. Even better – it takes little to no time to apply these tips to your studies!

Higher Degree of OOPs Concepts Level:

Merely learning about the definitions of class, object, inheritance, polymorphism, interface, an abstract class, etc., is not enough.

You must have a thorough, crystal-clear knowledge of OOPs concepts; and a complete understanding of their purpose uses and proper utilization; in order to write a maintainable and flexible, cost-effective quality software.

See below for some specific examples:

- You need to understand the exact purpose of OOPs components, such as abstract class, interface, method overriding, etc. If you cannot create or extend an object from an abstract class, then what is its purpose, etc.
- If an option occurs to choose between inheritance and encapsulation, you should know what the best option is.

- If an option occurs to choose between an abstract class and an interface as the code given below, then what is the best option and why?

```
interface Charger {
      void charge();
}
abstract class Charger {
      abstract void charge();
}
```

You should know why & how to write a flexible and maintainable code:

For example, in the working code below, the Board class' '*write*' method uses the BlueMarker class object. It has a bad code structure and is neither flexible nor maintainable.

```
class Board {
      public void write(BlueMarker m) {
            m.color();
   }
}
```

You should know how OOPs components such as interface and method overriding, etc., provide nicely extendable and flexible code. As well as understanding the consequences of bad code structure.

You should be able to identify the issues in code and make it right:

For example, can you identify the problem with this working code and convert it into a good one?

```
class Account {
      public double balance;
      public void withdraw () {
      }
}
```

You should have clear and definite clarifications of OOPs Concepts:

You may think that the encapsulation concept is just wrapping a field with a method. This is just an example of encapsulation, not the concept in fact.

The following questions will give you more ideas.

- How can an "interface" or an "abstract class", be used to aid in improving the degree of abstraction in the design of a class?
- Are both the concepts of encapsulation and abstraction really related to hiding complexities? Can you Justify your answer?
- How should we update a new version of an interface, so the existing client's code does not break?
- Both the composition and aggregation follow the Has-A relationship, then how are they different? Which one should you choose when?
- How can inheritance break the client code, but composition cannot? Illustrate the scenario example of this.

Do companies expect this level from a fresher?

No, this level of expertise comes with real-time implementation and experience.

But knowing this will makes you stand-out from others in an interview.

Just think...

If IT companies could get industry level or experienced level skills from a fresher – of course, they would hire you!

When I taught this level of skills to my candidates, they had an outstanding performance in interviews and obtained job offers quickly.

How can a Fresher Achieve this Level?

A fresher can achieve this level easily and quickly. I have made it surprisingly simple with my published book ***"OOP Concepts Booster"***. The book is available on Amazon worldwide and Flipkart.

This book is language agonistic and based on purely OOPs concepts with very simple code. The code syntax is in java, but the C# and other languages users can also understand it easily.

This level of OOP concepts is experimented. I picked some fresher candidates and taught the OOP concepts up to this level and observed that they performed differently in a technical interview and secured jobs quickly!

TIP: SHOWCASE YOUR SKILLS AND WORK SAMPLES ONLINE.

Let your online work samples speak *for* you!

Showcasing your skills online is a powerful tool to dramatically boost your chances of getting interview calls and getting hired. It tells the recruiters more about you and your skills during the shortlisting of your resume, before attending an interview or during the technical interview. Showcasing your skills through work samples gives recruiters confidence in hiring you.

What kind of skills and work samples to showcase online?

Here are some ideas to help you understand about showcasing your work samples.

- You can solve algorithms, write technical articles and programs of your choice, etc.
- You can create projects and applications. It does not matter if the project is big or small.

You have hidden talent and you can prepare your work samples easily. Just you need to start thinking creatively and act. I will be elaborating on it a little, but first, learn where you can keep your work samples online to showcase them.

Where to showcase my work samples?

Here are some of the ways you can showcase your work samples online and provide the links in your resume.

- Social media platforms like LinkedIn and Quora. You can write your technical articles and post on them.

- You can create projects, programs, or applications, etc. and place them on the GitHub repository.
- You can create your own website by buying your own domain and hosting from hosting providers. Create your portfolio and post your skills out there.

NOTE:

1. It is known that some fresh graduates create projects and only talk about these in their application or interview. This is not giving graduates the best chance of their talent being noticed; you should present your talents online as well as showcasing them through your resume.
2. To ensure clarity for the employer, you must provide the links to this showcase on the relevant section on your resume. The best place to put this section in your resume is just after the Key Skills section. Check out the Naukri and Linked for the facility to provide links for your work samples.

As an example, here are some of the work samples that I provide in my resume i.e. links to my published book 'OOP Concepts Booster' and website.

> My published book "OOP Concepts Booster": https://www.amazon.in/OOP-Concepts-Booster-Coding-Skills/dp/1647336805/
>
> My online work sample: https://www.interviewsansar.com/

Is creating your work sample online sounds difficult for you?

Believe me, it's easy!

Just you need to act and start.

The simple trick is, whatever program, you learn and practice from any of your related topics, compose them nicely with explanation, important points, etc, and post them on your social media profile, Quora website, etc. You can create a page on social media as well and post your article.

Start creating and posting a technical article of your choice. Try creating a simple project, even a very small, keep them on a repository like Github.

Don't think if they are perfect on the first go, just make sure they are correct. Update them if you feel it is required.

WARNING

Do not Copy Paste from other websites; you will be wasting your time. Any work presented should be 100% yours.

REMINDER

Place all your work samples links in your resume just after the key/ technical skills section.

TIP: WRITE CODE WITH COMMENTS AND MEANINGFUL NAMES OF VARIABLES AND FUNCTIONS.

This is not expected from a fresh graduate, but if you do this small and simple activity, it will show your maturity level as a coder and it will separate you from the crowd.

In an interview (or whatever it is: a coding test online or offline, or during a technical interview), whenever you write code, **write the meaningful names of variables and functions.**

Secondly, **always write code comments** before a function, or a complex line inside a method, for better understanding.

These will indicate to the interviewers that you have a good coding habit, which is a very important part of project and coding standards. Having good coding practices makes it easy to understand other people's code.

Here I will show you a bad example of variable and method naming conventions, and a good example that includes good naming conventions and code comments to get you an idea.

The primary intent is to showcase that you have a mindset of writing good code and code comments.

Here are the bad and good examples.

Consider the example, you need to write a function custom quick sort to improve its performance.

These are the pseudo-code example for illustration purposes only.

Bad example:

This example neither contains the meaningful name of the function and variables nor any code comments.

```
void cqs(int elements[], int n)

{

        int l,r;

        int b=20;


        if( n < b){

                insertionSort( elements, n);

        }else{

                quicksort(elements, l, r);

        }

}
```

Next, have a look at a good example.

Good example:

This example is a self-readable code and contains comments and meaningful names of the variables and the function.

```
/*This function provides the best performance using inser-
tion sort and quick sort algorithms.
For a lower set of data input, it will use
the insertion sort O(n2) technique as it performs
better than the quick sort O(n log n).
*/


void customeQuickSort(int elements[], int numberOfEle-
ments)

{
        int leftMostElement, rightMostElement;
        int BOUNDARY=20;

        //Use insertion sort if the number of
```

```
        //elements is less that around 20 or
        //else quick sort
        if( numberOfElements < BOUNDARY){
             insertionSort( elements, numberOfElements);
        }else{
             quicksort(elements,       leftMostElement,
right- MostElement);
        }
}
```

NOTE

Many variables are involved in coding practice and a single alphabet is also used, but this is out of scope to discuss here. The primary intent to discuss is to show your intent of writing comments with a meaningful name of the variable and functions.

Another benefit of writing good code is, when you write the solution for a given coding problem in an interview, it helps you not to mess up the code and avoid confusion.

As per observation, one of my candidates as a fresher was specifically appreciated for it in an interview and was selected. He was given a coding problem to solve and submit online and he had written well-documented code with a meaningful name of variables and methods with nice code comments. It was reflecting like a production code of a project.

TIP: MENTION IN YOUR RESUME'S SUMMARY THAT YOU'RE FAMILIAR WITH THE OBJECT- ORIENTED DESIGN PRINCIPLES AND DESIGN PATTERNS.

The knowledge of object-oriented design principles and design patterns is also typically not expected from a fresh graduate. However, this is a very important variable that can separate you from other candidates.

Learn 2 to 3 design patterns and the SOLID OOP design principles and put them in your resume's summary section stating you are familiar with the basic object-oriented design principles and design patterns as given below as an example.

"Familiar with design principles (SOLID) and design patterns like Singleton, Factory, and Observer, etc."

It gives interviewers an impression of your highly mature mindset for writing code, as well as building flexible and maintainable software.

I would suggest that you learn the SOLID object-oriented design principles and Singleton, Factory, and Observer design patterns, as these are easy to understand. Try to implement an example and code for them, and to memorize just the names of the other design patterns.

Does this topic sound complex to you? Believe me, it's easy. It just needs you to act.

WARNING:

1. Don't claim that you are master of these design patterns and principles. Be honest and show the intent to an interviewer that you are just familiar with them.
2. These topics are very interesting, and you may start getting into it, but do not try to understand all the design patterns while you are in your first job search process. If you are still studying in college and have time, you may learn all of them.

Here is the list of principles and patterns for your reference:

SOLID Principles:

These OOP Design principles provide flexible and maintainable code.

S - Single Responsibility Principle

O - Open-Close Principle

L - Liskov Substitution Principle

I - Interface Segregation Principle

D - Dependency Interview Principle

Design Patterns:

Design patterns are used to solve recurring problems.

Creational	Structural	Behavioral
-Singleton -Factory -Abstract Factory -Prototype -Builder	-Bridge -Decorator -Adapter -Composite -Façade -Proxy -Flyweight	-Observer -State -Strategy -Visitor -Template method -Iterator -Memento -Mediator -Interpreter -Command -Chain of Responsibility

(Visit FAQ and study resources section of this book)

GENERAL

The tips in this section are basics and quite general things that we miss focusing on while preparing for a job interview, even though they are very important and powerful. Most fresh graduates chase interview calls rather than preparation, run after big brand IT companies, and probably misuse social media, wasting their crucial time. Thus, I thought it would be nice to share these general, yet effective tips that will help you in your job interview preparation.

Tips you'll learn:

- TIP: All you need are a few interview calls.
- TIP: Don't run after the big companies only.
- TIP: Attend job interviews even though you are on training or self-study.
- TIP: Don't misuse social media; save your time for preparing for job interviews.
- TIP: Review your day every night.
- TIP: Consider making notes on your related topics.

TIP: ALL YOU NEED ARE A FEW INTERVIEW CALLS.

The question may be on some minds reading this: how many interview calls do I really need? How many times on average before I get a job?

This is minus other calls for internships, training, or unrelated to your job profile. I am talking about the only interview calls related to your job profile such as developer or tester etc.

From my experience and keen observation, you need 7 interview calls maximum if you are very prepared.

Why do 7 interview calls maximum?

After the first few interviews without getting hired, you should analyze your weaknesses and work on them.

Have it at the back of your mind that you have limited time. Do all you can to assess your weaknesses and focus on making yourself better for your next interview. You should ask yourself, why am I failing? How can I do better? How can I nail my next interview?

Here's my experience in this regard...

I once trained a candidate who was two months fresh out of college. I trained him rigorously and unfortunately, due to this, he became a bit overconfident.

He would go into interviews bragging to the interviewers about how he knows this and knows that, and would even cut off the interviewer in the middle of a question and say "I know the answer."

I kept wondering why he was being rejected all the time.

After a while, I found out what he did during the interviews and told him how wrong it was. It wasn't very wise to walk into an interview with overconfidence. I told him that even if he knew the answer, he should wait for the interviewer to finish before giving it.

He should never brag about knowing too much, as that always turns companies off. They would see him as a terrible employee who couldn't work well with others, and he would come off as pompous or arrogant, and interviewers don't like that. I taught him a more humble and feasible approach to interviews, and he learned and decided to take my advice.

Just at his next interview, after correcting his previous mistakes, he bagged the job!

I have trained several other candidates like that, and they all bagged their jobs within 5-7 interviews. Yours should not be different.

TIP: DON'T RUN AFTER THE BIG COMPANIES ONLY.

The problem with most candidates is that they are so focused on working for big brand companies, and they only target big IT firms like TCS, WIPRO, and CAPGEMINI. Some even go as far as Google and Facebook.

Now, of course, there is nothing wrong with targeting big brands. It's absolutely amazing. But if this is your only plan, your only course of action, and you are straight-jacketed, you may lose out big!

You must realize that there are other brands and companies which are great! When you target big brands and lose out and continue targeting them, you may be losing big opportunities in other firms.

So be diverse, turn your focus to other alternatives.

The goal isn't to work for a BIG firm, the goal is to work for a good IT firm that pays well and gives you experience. Don't ignore them.

You should also know about these companies before working for them. Do your research on their websites, and even in the interview, you may ask them questions too.

TIP: ATTEND JOB INTERVIEWS EVEN THOUGH YOU ARE ON TRAINING OR SELF-STUDY.

Don't ever procrastinate on attending job interviews. It is never too early.

Don't ever think you'll definitely start interviewing when you finish your preparation.

You may think you don't need to attend job interviews yet if you are doing self-study or attending a training institute, so you stall on interviews. You are making a big mistake. Why?

Well, what is your ultimate goal? To land a good job or complete training or study?

Of course, the goal is to get a job, so start attending interviews!

You may also think "I don't know anything; how do I attend interviews without knowing anything about it?", or "What are the benefits of attending interviews without preparation? Wouldn't it just be a waste of time?". The list goes on.

Well, several factors are involved in being successful in interviews, and you never know just what the panel is looking for. You are only going to definitely be unsuccessful if you don't go at all! Here are the reasons why you should attend job interviews even though you are still in training or self-study.

1. You don't know which factors the company could select you on.

There are many factors you cannot predict with regards to the way a company could select you.

Some companies tend to have specific and exclusive training for candidates. They may go with aptitude tests, or tests to measure basic IQ and reasoning skills, basic programming skills, etc.

On the other hand, some companies may be in dire need of hiring competent staff, and for one reason or another, they may not have much time to do so. They might be running out of the resources (candidates) for their current or upcoming projects. They could select you and train you in the shortest possible time to get you ready for their projects. This is how unpredictable this system is.

There are several factors these companies take into consideration. You'll never know unless you try.

The bottom line is to be regular with your training or self-study for job preparation. Meanwhile, you should also start attending interviews.

To train yourself is vital, but your focus should be on the ultimate goal: to get a job.

2. **You will learn what questions are asked in the interviews and will become aware of your weak points.**

   You may realize that, even if you are not well-versed in the topics that the panel questions you about, you can at least gain an idea of what to expect during interviews. For example, someone interviewing for a Java development profile will require prior preparation and research on the kinds of questions that will be asked of such a candidate, in order to adequately prepare for the interview. You could also focus on your weaker skills, using them as areas for improvement.

3. **You will boost your confidence and remove your hesitation and shyness.**

   It's natural to be nervous at the initial stages of an interview, but as you progress in the course of said interview, you'll gradually feel a level of comfort and confidence building up.

Bonus tip:

In your resume, you should include the topics of the profiles that you want to attend interviews for and could be gaining training in, even if you are not yet fully prepared in them. It may be true that these are not your strongest topics, but you should still include them in your resume because ultimately you are going to learn these topics during your preparation. *So, don't wait, and start attending interviews alongside your training or self-study.*

TIP: DON'T MISUSE SOCIAL MEDIA; SAVE YOUR TIME FOR PREPARING FOR JOB INTERVIEWS.

Social media is an incredibly powerful tool that can help you in many aspects. However, you should not misuse it, otherwise, you might end up wasting a tremendous amount of time, and this will affect your preparation for job interviews and delay you in getting a job.

Unfortunately, most people only waste time on social media. Although social media can be very distracting sometimes, it is important to realize that it can be a truly powerful and strategic tool. All you have to do is use it well.

I remember when I was working with some candidates who, as expected, weren't using social media well. As students, they had used social media only for fun. Hence, as fresh graduates, they were still wasting time on social media, which could be very harmful to their careers.

It is important that, instead of wasting your time watching pointless videos, you focus on your preparation.

Now, I am not suggesting that you delete all your social media accounts and keep off social media. What I mean is that you should use social media well and timely. You should analyze how much time you might be wasting and work on it.

Also, look at it this way: when you eventually land a job, you will be able to spend as much time as your work allows you on social media; but right now you need to focus on your career!

TIP: REVIEW YOUR DAY EVERY NIGHT.

Reviewing your day every night before going to bed is a very effective method to keep you focused on your goal. It will help you to be productive. Every night you should spend at least 10 minutes reviewing your day. It does not matter what you did if you watched a movie, went outside, gossiped with friends, or did preparation for a job or anything. Analyze what contributes to you landing your dream job.

Once you analyze your day, imagine how fulfilled you will feel after getting that dream job, what happiness you and your parents will get, what lifestyle you will get, and so on, once you get a job.

The major benefits you will get with this activity is the focus. It will make you focus on your goal and will force you to act.

TIP: CONSIDER MAKING NOTES ON YOUR RELATED TOPICS.

Consider making a neatly organized, summarized, and easy to revise notes for important, tricky points and always good examples for each topic.

It will help you in your revision from time to time. It will help you revise the moments before an interview. It is honestly a great time saver. It is human nature to forget some percentage of things we've read after sometimes. For example,

If you pick a new topic, read the concepts, and understand deeply by using books, google, or other mediums. And you do research on that for hours without creating notes, after some time, maybe a month, you will find that you have forgotten a maximum percentage of the important points. Again, you need to refer to the books, google again, and invest some more time. I don't know if this happens to you, but it surely happens to me.

So, I have found that creating a note will speed up the revision that goes into your permanent memory and it will also help gain huge confidence. ***Please create notes!***

FOCUS WORDS

1. As per observations, most of the fresh graduates sought after getting interview calls in order to get a job, **but only a few of them focus on the job preparation that is necessary to help them acquire a job.** If you do not focus on effectively preparing your skill sets, many interviews will come and go, and you will get nowhere. You only need a few interviews calls to get a job. So, pay extra attention to your job preparation and invest your valuable time in job preparation.
2. Work on creating work samples online which highlight your skills and share it with recruiters via your resume, cover letter, and job portals. This is one of the powerful tools which will set you apart from the crowd. Additionally, if you fall short in some of the education requirements or there is a gap in your employment history, this tool will assist you in securing your first job.

HIGHLIGHTS: REVISION

1. Make your resume clean and concise by placing a **descriptive summary** of your background and a **list of key skills** on top of your resume, below the header with your contact information.
2. Use skill keywords related to your area of interest or your job profile so that your resume will have good visibility to recruiters and to job search engines.
3. Prepare a cover letter in advance and include it in your job application.
4. Log in to job portals frequently to make recruiters and job search engines aware that you are looking for a job.
5. Prepare a good presentation to respond to "Tell me about yourself", write it down and practice reading it aloud.
6. Answer each question with an example and in detail during a technical interview.
7. Always pose a question if the interviewer asks, "Do you have any questions for me?" Never answer it with a plain "No."
8. Completely eliminate thoughts about the saturation of the IT job market from your mind.
9. You need to receive only a few interview calls that match your profile to get a job. So, focus on improving your technical skills.
10. Pick one programming language of your interest and master it (acquire a deeper knowledge of it). Take your OOP concepts to the next level with the book "OOP Concepts Booster".
11. Focus on Coding Round (data structure and algorithms). **Practice every day**.
12. Showcase your skills and work samples online and include links to it in your resume.
13. Don't run after the big companies only.
14. Review your day every night before you sleep. It will help you to be productive.

TOP HIRING MODELS

Many fresher candidates want to know about hiring models. They have a question if it is good to get a job through a job consultancy also termed as a recruitment agency etc.? Does a candidate need to pay or not for the job to consultants etc? or what is the referral for the hiring process? or what is outsourcing?

You might be familiar, but it is important to clarify to others. So, they do not have any confusion and act in the right direction quickly. Let me explain to you briefly about some top hiring models viz direct recruitment from the company, employee referrals, via job agencies, and outsourcing.

Direct recruitment from the company

The IT companies' HR finds candidates from different sources such as job portals and social media etc. conduct walk-ins, interviews, select the right candidates, and hire them.

Through Referrals

The companies open vacancies internally on their job portals and ask their employees to refer candidates.

The employees search candidates in their relatives, friends, and social group, etc and refer a candidate's resume to the company. Then the company shortlists and interview candidates for the hiring process.

The employee may get some bonus money or rewards for referring a candidate.

Through a Jab Consultancy

Some of the IT companies do not invest time and money for themselves to find and shortlist candidates.

They ask job consultancy companies to find the right candidates and schedule interviews with them. The company selects the candidates by interviewing them. Once the candidates are hired, the company pays money to the job consultancies.

It should be noted that neither the company nor the jab consultants ask candidates for the money.

Through Outsourcing

Some IT companies hire candidates from an outsourcing company. The outsourcing companies hire candidates on their payroll and send them to other IT companies (known as client-side) to work as per demand.

So, you don't have any issue with attending interviews in outsourcing companies as well.

FAQ & Study Resources

You might have some general questions in your mind regarding a job or interviews in the IT industry such as given below:

Q) Can a fresher negotiate salary?

Q) Does the programming language I have learned need a certification to get a job?

Q) Is it compulsory to have 60% in 10th, 12th, and graduation to get a job in the IT industry? Or most of the IT companies ask for 60% what should I do?

Q) Does personality matter in an IT company even you are best at coding?

Q) If I don't know the answer to some of the questions, can it be a reason for rejection?

and **what are the good study resources** like websites, books, and YouTube, etc to learn the topics for the job interview preparation?

To get the answers and details, you can visit the website https:// www.interviewsansar.com. In the footer (bottom of the website's page) you will find a link for freshers FAQs and study resources.

I thought not to include the FAQ and study resources here in this book itself but on my website in order to keep you updated with the latest information or something. Moreover, there may be more user questions or some upcoming more good resources for study.

About the Author

Rakesh Singh is a highly experienced software professional and is passionate about designing and developing quality software. He is also a coding lover and an expert in OOP concepts besides multiple programming languages such as C, C++, Java, and C# and has been coding for decades. He is a technical blogger and manages his blog on https://www.interviewsansar.com, where he shares his skills with the world.

He has taken tons of interviews of freshers and experienced candidates as a technical panel in the hiring process and given quality candidates to organizations.

Author other Books

www.ingramcontent.com/pod-product-compliance
Lightning Source LLC
LaVergne TN
LVHW100309210926
848480LV00003B/1073
* 9 7 9 8 9 0 5 1 0 8 8 8 4 *